THEN AND THERE SERIES
GENERAL EDITOR
MARJORIE REEVES M.A. PH.D.

D1635583

The Chartists

PETER

Illustrated from contemporary sources

WORKING MEN'S COLLEGE
31948

LONGMAN

LONGMAN GROUP LTD
LONDON
Associated companies, branches and representatives
throughout the world

© Peter Searby 1967

All rights reserved. No part of this
publication may be reproduced, stored
in a retrieval system, or transmitted
in any form or by any means, electronic,
mechanical, photocopying, recording, or
otherwise, without the prior permission
of the Copyright owner.

First published 1967

Second impression 1968

Third impression 1970

SBN 582 20408 9

ACKNOWLEDGEMENTS

We are grateful to Macmillan & Co. Ltd. for permission to include an
extract from *British Working Class Movements: Selected Documents 1789–
1875*, edited by G. D. H. Cole and A. W. Filson.

Also we should like to record our gratitude to the many people who
gave their help and advice in the preparation of this book, and in
particular to the following: Mrs M. E. Cunnington, Mr D. J. Davis,
Miss G. H. Shillito and Mr W. G. Wyman in the teaching services of
Coventry, Birmingham, and Warwickshire; Mr W. Broadfield of
Leicester Reference Library, Mr G. A. Chinnery, City Archivist for
Leicester, and Mr John Daniel of Leicester City Museum; and Mrs
Searby.

For permission to reproduce photographs we should like to thank the
following: *The Guardian Journal*, Nottingham—page 72; Guildhall
Library—cover and pages 20, 36 and 37; *Illustrated London News*—
pages 38, 39, 43, 44, 45, 63 and 64; E. Kirby, Esq.—pages 51 and 53;
Leicester City Libraries—pages 22, 34 and 40; Leicester Museum—
pages 2, 4, 15, 16 and 76; The National Library of Wales—page 80;
The National Monuments Record—page 57; Radio Times Hulton
Picture Library—pages 9, 12, 59, 61, 62, 65, 77 and 84; Punch—
pages 66 and 67.

The map on page 7 is redrawn from A. T. Patterson, *Radical Leicester*,
by kind permission of the Leicester University Press; the map on page
58 is Crown Copyright Reserved.

PRINTED IN MALTA BY ST PAUL'S PRESS LTD

CONTENTS

TO THE READER

No families in Britain today have to live on 4s 6d a week, or to beg used tea-leaves from neighbours to make a drink. In the 1830s and 1840s many people were as poor as this, even when they had jobs. They were often out of work and then they were poorer still. The Poor Law, which was supposed to look after them when they were unemployed, was harsh and cruel. If they tried to raise their wages by joining trade unions their employers and the government sometimes attacked them.

These men thought that they could make their lives richer and happier only if they controlled the government. To do this they needed votes, and at that time poor men did not often have votes. The People's Charter of 1838 demanded that all men should have votes. The men who supported the Charter were called Chartists.

This book is mainly about the Chartists in one town, Leicester, and is based on books by historians of the present day and on writings of Chartist times—reports in newspapers and books written by Chartists and people who knew them. You will find a list of these writings on p. 92. There may be similar ones from your town. You should remember while you are reading this book that there were Chartists in nearly every town, and that a good deal of what happened in Leicester happened in other towns too—perhaps in yours.

THE SIX POINTS OF THE PEOPLE'S CHARTER
(Summary of the People's Charter, taken from a poster of the time.)

1. A VOTE for every man twenty-one years of age, of sound mind, and not undergoing punishment for crime.
2. THE BALLOT. To protect the elector in the exercise of his vote.
3. NO PROPERTY QUALIFICATION for members of Parliament—thus enabling the *constituencies** to return the man of their choice, be he rich or poor.
4. PAYMENT OF MEMBERS, thus enabling an honest tradesman, working man, or other person, to serve a constituency, when taken from his business to attend to the interests of the country.
5. EQUAL CONSTITUENCIES, securing the same amount of representation for the same number of electors—instead of allowing small constituencies to swamp the votes of larger ones.
6. ANNUAL PARLIAMENTS, thus presenting the most effectual check to bribery and intimidation, since though a constituency might be bought once in seven years (even with the ballot), no purse could buy a constituency (under a system of universal suffrage) in each ensuing twelvemonth; and since members, when elected for a year only, would not be able to defy and betray their constituents as now.

* Words printed like this are included in the glossary on page 95.

PRICES IN CHARTIST TIMES

Prices were a lot lower in the 1830s and 1840s than they are today. Usually, 5s would buy what 35s would today. This means that you have to multiply sums of money by seven to find out their value today. Of course, wages were a lot lower too.

In the 1830s and 1840s a four-pound loaf usually cost between $5\frac{1}{2}d$ and 7d, butter about 1s 6d or 1s 7d a pound, cheese 7d or 8d a pound, cheap tea 4s a pound, and potatoes 3s a hundredweight. The cheapest fat bacon could cost as little as 2d or 3d a pound but good steak often cost over 1s a pound; this was why poor people did not usually eat meat. Soap and candles cost about 7d or 8d a pound, while the same amount of money would in Leicester buy a hundredweight of coal. Places further away from coalmines would have to pay more for it.

1   Thomas Cooper Comes to Leicester

In November 1840 Thomas Cooper, a journalist, came to Leicester to work on the 'Leicester Mercury'. One of his first jobs was to report on a Chartist meeting. He had read about Chartists, but he had never talked to one or been to a Chartist meeting. So at this one he listened carefully to the speaker telling the audience to 'Stick to your Charter. You are slaves without your votes.' Cooper wanted to know why the Chartists were so eager for the vote, and after the meeting he walked home with some Chartists and asked them about their lives. In Leicester many men were weavers and Cooper asked how much a weaver earned.

'About four and sixpence,' was the answer.

'Four and sixpence,' Cooper said. 'Well, six fours are twenty-four, and six sixpences are three shillings. That's seven and twenty shillings a week. The wages are not so bad when you are in work.' (Remember to multiply by seven to see what twenty-seven shillings would be worth today.)

Cooper did not expect the reply he got.

'What are you talking about?' said they. 'You mean four and sixpence a day. But we mean four and sixpence a week.'

'Four and sixpence a WEEK!' exclaimed Cooper. 'You don't mean that men have to work a whole week for four and sixpence? How can they maintain their wives and children?'

'Ay, you may well ask that,' said one of the Chartists.

Cooper afterwards wrote that this conversation was the first thing 'that revealed to me the real state of suffering in which thousands in England were living'. It made him a Chartist.

2　How the Weavers Lived

Thomas Cooper found that the weavers lived in tiny cottages.
Here is a photograph of a weaver's cottage built about 1820

*A Street in Hinckley photographed in 1870, looking as it had done in Chartist times.
The building on the extreme left was a weaver's cottage. It had one room downstairs
and one bedroom. Notice the shop, the pump and the cobbled street.*

in Hinckley, near Leicester. How does it compare in size with
an ordinary modern house? The rent of a cottage like this was
about 2s 6d a week and this left very little for food. Many
weavers' families lived on bread and potatoes, with an ounce

of coffee a week as a special luxury. Some could not afford even this. In the 1870s a weaver called Daniel Merrick wrote a short book about a weaver's family in Chartist times. The father worked eighty hours a week but still could not afford tea.

'The oldest girl, Mary Ann, was sent to Mrs Kindheart, the landlady of the "Horse and Trumpet", to ask whether she would give them some tea leaves, and having obtained them, they would be used over again by the family. Some bread would complete the meal. Very little meat ever entered the house, unless it was a pennyworth of liver or three-halfpennyworth of fat. Frequently on Saturdays there was no dinner at all because the money was gone. For clothes they depended on charity from ladies and gentlemen in the neighbourhood.'

The Leicester weavers made all kinds of things—shirts, scarves, braces, gloves and, most of all, woollen stockings. These were knitted on complicated machines called stocking-frames and the men who worked these were called stocking-weavers, framework-knitters or stockingers. The knitter worked the frame with his hands and feet; he had no steam engine to help his muscles. Many stockingers worked at home and kept their frames there. If you look at the photograph of a weaver's cottage you will see that the downstairs windows are large. Can you guess why?

Framework-knitters made stockings for *hosiers*, most of whom were rich men. The knitters who worked at home collected their *yarn* from the hosier's warehouse on Monday morning and brought the finished stockings back on Saturday. They were then paid. The stockingers often did no work on Mondays and the hosiers called them lazy for taking a day's holiday. The weavers made up for it the rest of the week. They rose at five or six, or in summer as soon as it was light; they were then at their frames till ten or eleven at night, from Tuesday to Friday. Soon after coming to Leicester, Cooper was very surprised to see 'the long upper windows of the cottages fully lighted, and to hear the loud creak of the stocking-frame',

Leicester stockinger photographed in 1880.

at eleven p.m. The weavers would knit for seventy hours a week, or perhaps even eighty like Mary Ann's father. Mary Ann and her brothers and sisters worked very hard too, seaming the stockings and winding the woollen yarn on to bobbins. Children of four or five did this for twelve hours a day. The *commissioners* who came to find out how the workers lived in Leicester in 1833 said that the stockingers' children were worse off than those in factories. They worked longer hours and their health was bad. They were 'miserable, dirty, hungry and wretched'.

The stockingers were paid a few pence for every dozen pairs of stockings they knitted and they could make seven or eight shillings' worth in a week when they had enough work. But from this money other amounts were deducted. Most stockingers could not afford to own frames and rented them from hosiers for about 1s 6d a week. The frameworkers had to pay fines if the hosiers said there were faults in their knitting. Often the 'faults' didn't exist. Some hosiers kept shops and

A hosier's house: Enderby Hall, near Leicester

paid their workers in tokens which could be spent only in their shops, where the prices were always higher than elsewhere. This was called 'paying truck'.

Some hosiers put their frames together in workshops and the

stockingers who worked in them were the worst off. Every spare piece of floor had a frame on it and the knitters could hardly move about. They still had to pay frame-rent, and even rent for the space the frame took up on the floor! They had to buy the oil and needles for their frames, lights for the darker months and coal for the fire. They had to pay somebody to seam their stockings and wind the bobbins. Often this would be done by an old man too weak to work a frame, who earned a few shillings seaming and winding.

The stockingers went on strike many times for higher wages. One of the longest strikes was from December 1833 to May 1834, but this failed like all the others, and in the end the weavers had to return to work without gaining anything.

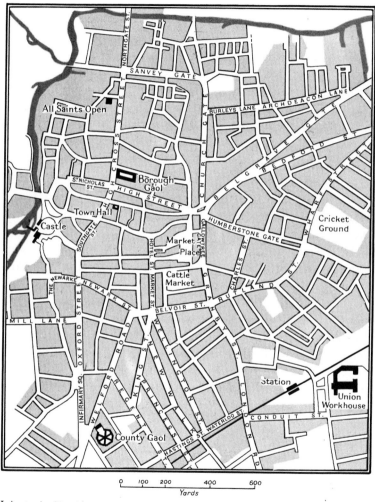

Leicester in Chartist times

3 The New Poor Law and the People's Charter

In each parish in England certain men, usually called 'overseers of the poor', paid a few shillings a week to very poor people who otherwise would have starved. Quite often this money was paid to men who were unemployed. This happened in Leicester. There and in some other towns the money was also paid to men like Mary Ann's father, who had jobs but didn't earn enough at them. This money was called 'poor relief', and the overseers got it by charging rates on the value of all houses and land in the parish. If a man had a house worth £20 and the rate was 5s in the pound he would have to pay £5 a year in poor rates.

In 1831 £7,000,000 was paid in poor rates in England and Wales, most of it by people a lot richer than a Leicester stocking-knitter. The ratepayers thought the bill was too high. Parliament agreed with them, and in 1834 passed an Act, the Poor Law Amendment Act, which was intended to lower it. In future everybody except the old and sick who wanted poor relief was to have to go into a *workhouse* to get it. 'Outdoor' relief (that is, relief given to people who lived outside the workhouse) was to stop, and the workhouses were to be made unpleasant, so that poor people would want to stay outside and thus not spend the ratepayers' money.

The new workhouses were grim brick buildings, painted inside in the gloomiest of colours. The food was meagre and dull; *paupers* were sometimes fed for less than a shilling a head a week. The diet was intended to keep them in health so that they would be fit for work when they left, but sometimes it did not do even this. In the Andover workhouse the paupers had to work all day breaking bones. (Hard monotonous work was part of the workhouse discipline everywhere.) They were so badly fed that they fought each other for the rotting gristle that was stuck to the horses' bones.

A workhouse in the 1840s: the room for men and boys. Notice the straw, used for sleeping on

Above all, paupers were deliberately made to feel that they were criminals, not unfortunate men and women who deserved to be fed and housed properly. Families were split—children from their parents and parents from each other. Nothing about the New Poor Law was hated more than this. One poor law official himself said that 'the object in building these workhouses was to establish a discipline so severe and repulsive as to make them a terror to the poor and prevent them from entering'.

9

The government thought that if the poor were deterred in this way they would be forced to find work. But the poor knew that the New Poor Law would force them to choose, when there was a *slump*, between starving and going into something like a prison. When the new system was started in 1836 and 1837 there was a bad slump which led to a good deal of unemployment in the North and Midlands. In Leicester the Poor Law Guardians opened a new workhouse for about 500 paupers early in 1838. They then started the harsh new system—stopping outdoor relief and separating men and women in the workhouse.

Hating poverty and the New Poor Law the Leicester stockingers did what the poor elsewhere did. Like the cotton-weavers of Lancashire and the woollen-weavers of Yorkshire, the nail-makers of the Black Country and the coalminers of Newcastle, they demanded the political power that they did not have. Very few poor men had ever had votes or had been able to sit in Parliament. Many had hoped that the 1832 Reform Bill would give them votes but it had in fact given votes only to quite comfortably-off men like farmers and shopkeepers. In England only about 600,000 men out of 3,000,000 over the age of twenty-one had votes. Very large towns like Leicester with 40,000 inhabitants had two M.P.s, as did small ones like Chippenham. M.P.s were not paid and poor men were also kept out of the House of Commons by a law which said that an M.P. had to own a lot of property. General elections were held once every seven years and many people felt that this was not often enough. Voters had to vote (or 'ballot') in public and this often meant that they lost their jobs or houses if they did not vote the way their employers or landlords wanted. In Leicester the hosiers threatened to take away the frames of awkward stockingers.

In 1838 some London *Radicals*, the most important being William Lovett, published the People's Charter, named after the Great Charter of 1215. The new Charter was written as a Bill that the Radicals hoped to get Parliament to pass. (You will find some quotations from the Charter on p. v.) The Charter called for manhood *suffrage*, annual parliaments, equal *electoral districts*, payment of M.P.s, the abolition of the property qualification for M.P.s, and the secret ballot. All over Britain men demanded the Six Points of the Charter. The Chartist movement was born.

It might seem odd that people who were poor should want votes, not more food or money. The Chartists, however, planned to use their power in Parliament, when they got it, to make their lives happier. A Lancashire Chartist, Joseph Rayner Stephens (you may read more about him on p. 81) said:

> 'This question of universal suffrage is a knife and fork question, a bread and meat question. If any man ask what I mean by universal suffrage, I mean to say that every working man in the land has a right to a good coat on his back, a good hat on his head, a good roof for the shelter of his household, a good dinner upon his table, no more work than will keep him in health while at it, and as much wages as will keep him in the enjoyment of plenty, and all the blessings of life that reasonable men could desire.'

The editor of the 'Leicester Chronicle' said that Chartism meant 'better wages, limited hours of labour, comfort, independence, happiness—all that the fond heart of suffering man pictures to him of joy and prosperity in his happiest moments'.

4   Feargus O'Connor

The most famous leader of the Chartists was Feargus
O'Connor. He was born in Ireland in 1796. His uncle Arthur

Feargus O'Connor

and his father Roger O'Connor fought against English rule in
Ireland. Arthur became a general in Napoleon's army and
Roger bought a large estate which he could not afford—to
accommodate Napoleon, he said, when he invaded England.
The upkeep of his house led him into two crimes—setting
fire to the house after insuring it for £5,000, and robbing the
Galway mail coach. He believed that he was descended from

the High King of Ireland in the eleventh century, and wrote a strange book about the early history of Ireland, which was said to be 'translated from the original manuscripts in the Phoenician dialect of the Scythian language'. These manuscripts did not exist. Roger died insane.

Feargus was to die insane too, and throughout his life he was always odd. He was boastful; he too talked of his descent from the ancient kings of Ireland. He was a very clever mimic and storyteller, but many of his stories were not true. His behaviour was impulsive and unpredictable. At school he was most interested in boxing, practical jokes and horse-racing. He was expelled after having a love affair with his schoolmaster's daughter.

Feargus became a Radical, speaking for the Roman Catholic peasants of Ireland against their English Protestant rulers, though he was a Protestant. He attracted reporters to his meetings by paying them three guineas for attending; in this way he got newspaper publicity. He was elected M.P. for County Cork in 1832 but three years later lost his seat when it was found that he did not own enough land to give him an income of £600 a year; this was necessary for M.P.s.

After this O'Connor gave more attention to the poor in England than in Ireland. He attacked the New Poor Law and became a Chartist. In November 1837 he began to publish a newspaper in Leeds, the 'Northern Star', which soon was the best known of the Chartist newspapers. O'Connor employed good correspondents and a brilliant *leader writer*, another Irishman, Bronterre O'Brien. By 1839 50,000 copies of the 'Northern Star' were sold each week, far more than any other paper published outside London. Fewer than 1,000 copies a week of each of the three Leicester papers were sold.

Mary Ann's brother William worked in a frame-shop as a bobbin-winder. There was a tea break at 5 o'clock before the long evening session, and during it 'some would seat themselves on the winders' stools, some on bricks. After tea a short article would be read from the 'Northern Star', and this would form the subject matter for consideration and chat during the remainder of the day.' In 1839 O'Connor made £13,000 profit from the 'Northern Star', but he spent money wildly and often did not have enough to pay the printers' wages.

O'Connor was over six feet in height, fat and broad-shouldered, with a round face and a very loud voice, red hair and fair skin. He could hold the attention of a huge crowd of Chartists for hours, making them angry over their poverty and the New Poor Law and then making them laugh with his jokes about the government.

5 The Beginning of Chartism in Leicester

Leicester in 1846. Notice the train and the prison, above the locomotive

In November 1838 the Leicester Chartists gathered to discuss the People's Charter and listen to Feargus O'Connor. It began to drizzle early in the morning and soon it was pouring with rain. Even so, 2,000 turned out. They marched in procession through the rain carrying flags with slogans embroidered on them—'No Poor Law Bill', 'The Rights of the People and Nothing Less', 'Liberty and Prosperity' and 'It is better to perish by the sword than by hunger'. Many of the Chartists were regular church-goers, and they often liked to sing hymns with a political flavour at their meetings. At this one they sang one by Ebenezer Elliott, the 'Corn Law Rhymer'. (The Chartists disliked the *Corn Laws* because they thought that they put up the price of bread.)

> 'God of the Poor! shall labour eat?
> Or drones alone find labour sweet?

Lo, they who call the earth their own,
Take all we have—and give a stone!

Lord! not for vengeance rave the wrong'd,
The hopes deferred, the woes prolonged;
Our cause is just, our Judge divine;
But judgment, God of all, is thine!'

O'Connor kept the crowd attentive for two hours with his attacks on the 'gingerbread mayor' of Leicester, England's 'fungus aristocracy' and the 'headless, brutal, brainless Poor Law Commissioners'. The government was like a man who can 'see black slavery across the Atlantic, and not see the white slavery under his own nose'. (Parliament had abolished slavery in the British Empire in 1833.)

In the evening 250 Chartists went to a dinner in Leicester Town Hall in O'Connor's honour. As he entered a band

Leicester Old Town Hall

played 'See the Conquering Hero Comes'. After the dinner of roast beef and the *toasts* and then two songs—'Millions be free' and 'Hearts of Oak'—O'Connor made a second speech, very like the one he had made in the morning. He enjoyed making speeches. A heckler interrupted him but O'Connor soon squashed him: 'My good fellow, if you don't discontinue that you must go out neck and crop'.

Chartist Land Colonies +

Newcastle on Tyne

Bradford
Leeds
Bolton
Ashton-u-Lyne
Manchester
Stalybridge
Liverpool
Gainsborough
Stockport
Sheffield
Lincoln
Crewe
Burslem
Newcastle-under-
Hanley
Nottingham
Lyme
Longton
Loughborough
Stafford
Stamford
Hinckley
Leicester
Birmingham
DODFORD+
Warwick
Bromsgrove
Northampton
LOWBANDS+
CHARTERVILLE
Merthyr
SNIG'S END+
+
Tydfil
Witney
Oxford
Newport
O'CONNORVILLE
Bristol
+
London
Tolpuddle

England and Wales in Chartist times, showing places mentioned in the book.

18

6   The National Convention, 1839

By the end of 1838 there were Chartists in nearly every town in Britain. The Birmingham Chartists suggested sending the House of Commons a request, a petition, asking it to carry out the People's Charter. One Birmingham man wrote that he wanted a 'petition signed by 2,000,000 men, drawn, like a Cheshire cheese of twenty feet diameter, in a cart of white horses to the House of Commons'. From Birmingham too came the idea of a meeting in London of *delegates* from Chartists in every town, to draw up the petition and present it to the House of Commons. Both these ideas were adopted.

The Leicester Chartists chose a schoolmaster called Thomas Smart as their delegate to the meeting. Smart was sixty-eight years old. Like many Chartists he had educated himself after only a few years at school. He knew Latin, French, Italian and Spanish and a lot about mathematics. He also wrote poetry. Besides teaching he drew plans of buildings for architects and made machinery.

The Chartist meeting began in February 1839, the same time as Parliament, in the British Coffee House, Cockspur Street, London. It was called the 'General Convention of the Industrious Classes' or the 'People's Parliament'; some of its members wrote after their names 'M.C.'—'Member of the Convention'. Preparing the petition took until May and even when it was ready Parliament did not consider it for two more months. In May the Convention moved to Birmingham. There they discussed what to do when Parliament rejected the petition, which it was quite certain to do.

Some of the Chartists (called 'moral force' Chartists) wanted to use only peaceful methods and said so. They hoped to persuade Parliament to grant the Charter and they expected

The Chartist Convention, 1839. Can you see O'Connor?

to have to go on persuading for years. Chief among the moral force Chartists was William Lovett. (You may read more about him on p. 84.) Most of the moral force Chartists soon left the Convention because they were disgusted with what the more violent delegates, the 'physical force' Chartists, were saying. One of them was George Julian Harney, aged twenty-two, who wore a red cap like the more violent men in the French Revolution to show how revolutionary he was, and waved a dagger at meetings. Harney wanted the workers of Britain to stage a general strike when the petition was rejected. The strikers would not be able to afford food and so would have to take it by force. An *insurrection* would follow. This would succeed. 'Before the end of the year, the people shall have universal suffrage or death.'

Feargus O'Connor was called a physical force Chartist too, and some of his words were just as wild as Harney's. He told one meeting at this time that 'physical force was treason only when it failed; it was glorious freedom when it was successful'. He asked the audience what it would do if members of the Convention were arrested. 'We'd rise,' replied the crowd, shouting for several minutes. 'Now,' said O'Connor, 'I'll stop; I'm hard of hearing—let me hear it again'. Again the audience yelled, 'We'd rise—we'd rise'.

But O'Connor and those who agreed with him (Smart was one) did not really want a rising at all. Their threats were meant to bluff the government into giving way. They knew that a revolution could not succeed. The Chartists might sometimes defeat soldiers in *guerrilla* fighting, as they did near Newcastle-under-Lyme in May; Chartists ambushed cavalry at night from behind barricades they had built in the streets. But sooner or later the Chartists would have to face soldiers in pitched battles and then they could never win because they did not have enough weapons or military training. As O'Connor said to the Convention, 'they would not be so foolish as to bare their naked bodies to disciplined soldiers'.

Parliament and the government knew this too and knew that O'Connor and his followers were bluffing. Despite the fact that it had been signed by 1,200,000 Chartists the petition was rejected by the House of Commons by a large majority in July. The Convention had then to decide after months of argument what to do next. It first decided to call a general strike (also called 'national holiday' or 'sacred month') to start on 12 August. Most of the delegates then had second thoughts. Many thousands of Chartists were unemployed already. Those who did have jobs would not want to risk them on a strike. In any case, a strike would probably lead to an insurrection which the army would crush. It would end 'in the utter subjection of the whole of the working class to the moneyed murderers of society'.

So the Convention called off the general strike, much to

Harney's disgust, and, instead, asked Chartists to stay off work for a few days to stage 'solemn processions and meetings', a 'great moral demonstration'. The general strike did not take place.

Chartism was 'hunger politics'. Chartists were most active and violent in the slump years of the 'Hungry Forties'—when wages were lowest and many thousands had no jobs at all. These years were 1839, 1842 and 1848.

In Leicester in 1839 people were dying of starvation and the 'Leicester Chronicle' spoke of the streets being full of a 'fearful army of gaunt and famishing men'. Families were by the winter pawning their last pieces of furniture, their mattresses and sheets, to get money for food. The Town Council thought the poor might riot and increased the number of policemen in

Leicester policemen in the 1840s, drawn by a schoolgirl at the time

the town from forty to fifty. They also recruited 150 *special constables*, and the Home Office sent 100 cutlasses and 100 pairs of pistols for them to use. The Home Secretary suggested that the *magistrates* should try to recruit special constables from among the retired soldiers or sailors living in Leicester on government pensions. The magistrates found, however, that most of them were too old, too ill, too drunken or too friendly with the Chartists to be useful.

On Whit Monday the Chartists held a meeting on some open land in Belvoir Street. A Chartist from Stalybridge in Cheshire, J. Deegan, told the audience: 'We will obtain our rights, peaceably if we can, forcibly if we must. If we cannot obtain them by fair means, we will obtain them by the bullet, the pike and the bayonet.' But the Leicester Chartist speakers disagreed with him. They were proud of being peaceful in Leicester and there were no riots in 1839.

Other towns were less peaceful. In Birmingham the police started the trouble. The first modern police force had only been started in 1828, in London, and as yet not every town had followed suit; Birmingham Town Council was too mean to pay for one. But when the Chartist Convention was meeting in Birmingham some *metropolitan* police were brought to the town by special train. On 4 July a large but peaceful crowd were listening to some Chartist speakers in the Bull Ring. The police, armed with cutlasses and clubs, attacked the crowd, which fought back. Soldiers had to restore order.

In Bolton and Newcastle-upon-Tyne the Chartists tried to start general strikes and there were pitched battles with policemen and soldiers. In Bolton the Chartists fought with guns and pikes for three days and destroyed the machinery in the cotton mills before they were beaten. In November there was a rising in South Wales (which you may read about on p. 79) and in January 1840 three in the West Riding of Yorkshire. The leader, Samuel Holberry, died in prison in 1842 after being kept in solitary confinement; at his funeral the mourners sang a hymn specially written by a Leicester Chartist stocking-weaver, John Henry Bramwich—'Great God, is this the patriot's doom?'

By June 1840 500 Chartist leaders were in prison for their share in the riots or for their *seditious* words at the Convention or elsewhere. O'Connor was among them. The first efforts of the Chartists had failed but the movement was not dead. It soon revived everywhere and in Leicester it was livelier than it had ever been. That this was so was largely due to one man —Thomas Cooper.

7 Thomas Cooper

Thomas Cooper, aged 65

Thomas Cooper's father died when he was four and afterwards he and his mother could afford to eat only potatoes.
When he was six a chimney sweep wanted to make him a
climbing boy; he was small enough to climb up sooty chimneys.
The sweep offered his mother two guineas as bribe; this was a
fortune to her and she was tempted, but Thomas's cries,
'Mammy, mammy, do not let the grimy man take me away'
changed her mind. Their poverty made Cooper a young
Radical. 'I hated the Liverpool government, and its master,
bitterly, and believed that the sufferings of the poor were
chiefly to be blamed on them.' (Lord Liverpool was the Prime
Minister from 1812 to 1827.) Thomas could read when he was
three, and at school he paid no fees but instead from the age of

eleven onwards taught the younger children. He liked playing the *dulcimer* and at eight could play any tune by ear. He drew pictures of lions, tigers and elephants when the circus came to Gainsborough, and collected birds' eggs and wild flowers. Most of all he enjoyed reading—Byron, Shakespeare, the voyages of Captain Cook and the stories of Bampfylde Moore-Carew, the King of the Gypsies.

After a short time as a sailor—nine days, which he hated—Cooper became a shoemaker when he was fifteen, and his education, so he says, really began. 'Mine has been almost entirely self-education all the way through life.' Cooper was very intelligent, with a vast memory and enormous energy which enabled him to work very hard. He kept his mother and himself on the 10s a week he earned making shoes. He rose at three or four in the morning and studied till seven, when work began. 'A book or a periodical in my hand while I breakfasted, gave me another half hour's reading. I had another half hour, and sometimes an hour's reading, or study of language, at from one to two o'clock, the time of dinner—usually eating my food with a spoon, after I had cut it in pieces, and having my eyes on a book all the time.' As he worked he memorised the rules of mathematics or Latin grammar. He made shoes till eight or nine in the evening, and then read poetry till he fell into bed exhausted. 'I not infrequently swooned away, and fell along the floor, when I tried to take my cup of oatmeal gruel, at the end of my day's labour.'

At twenty-three he began a private school and soon collected 100 pupils. Cooper worked in the school from five in the morning till nine at night, cutting *quill* pens and taking extra classes, like Latin, for the brightest children, when most of his pupils had gone home. He covered the walls with pictures and built little museums on each window sill for the boys' coins and pebbles. He was a very pious Wesleyan Methodist and unlike most schoolmasters in those days would not cane boys, because he felt that it was sinful. 'But one day, when I was faint and weak, I lost my temper with a very disobedient boy in the school, and suddenly seized the cane and struck him. The whole school seemed horror-stricken—I wished I was in a corner to weep, for I was choking with tears, and felt heart-broken.'

After a few years he left schoolteaching because he was impatient with slow boys and found no pleasure in teaching them. Throughout his life Cooper had great confidence in his own intelligence and opinions, and was proud, quick-tempered and quarrelsome. He could not suffer fools gladly and always wanted his own way. When he was nine he hit a boy on the head with a shovel for damaging his snowman.

Cooper quarrelled with the Methodists in Gainsborough and left for Lincoln; he quarrelled with them there too. He became a journalist and manager of a Stamford newspaper at the large salary of £300 a year, but soon resigned because the paper's owner would not give him enough power. He moved to London, had to pawn his belongings and sell his 500 books, but in 1840 became editor of a Greenwich newspaper at £150 a year. He quarrelled with the owner very soon and gave notice that he was leaving.

'But I had a letter from Lincoln, enclosing a letter from the manager of a Leicester paper, inquiring, "Can you inform us of the whereabouts of Thomas Cooper, who wrote the articles entitled 'Lincoln Preachers' in the 'Stamford Mercury'?"

'I dropped the letter from my hands; and my wife remembers well my excited state, as I exclaimed, "The message has come at last!—THE MESSAGE OF DESTINY! We are going to Leicester!".'

8 Thomas Cooper and the 'Shakespearean Chartists'

Cooper was invited to become a reporter on the 'Leicester Mercury' at £2 a week. But very soon after coming to Leicester he went to the meeting which as we know made him a Chartist. 'As I considered the Chartist side to be the side of the poor and suffering, I held up my hand for the Charter at public meetings. I was made of mettle that must take a side, and I could only take the side I did take.' He had thought of studying again in Leicester, but said, 'What is the acquirement of languages—what is the obtaining of all knowledge, compared to the real honour of struggling to win the rights of millions?'

He was soon dismissed from the 'Mercury' because of his Chartism. The Leicester Chartists had started their own newspaper—the 'Midland Counties Illuminator', and Cooper became its editor and put the energy that he had used in studying into making it pay. He had it printed on better paper,

Heading of the 'Midland Counties' Illuminator'. This was one of the first issues edited by Cooper

raised the price to $1\frac{1}{2}d$, and like a modern newspaper owner increased its circulation by advertising in the 'Northern Star'. An army of unemployed stockingers sold the 'Illuminator' in Leicester and villages nearby. Cooper made the paper prosper; he moved into larger offices in Church Street, where he also sold bread and had two rooms as a Chartist coffee bar.

In April 1841 Cooper became *secretary* of the Leicester Chartists. Soon he was calling himself 'general' and treating his band of followers as an army, giving 'Chartist commissions' to several grades of officers. Chartists who would not accept his bossy ways left. Cooper's followers met in a room in the Amphitheatre used as an actors' dressing-room and called the 'Shakespearean Room'. So they were called 'the Shakespearean Association of Leicester Chartists'. Cooper was still interested in music and poetry and wanted his men to have rousing tunes to sing as they marched. With two stockingers he wrote a book of Chartist hymns called the 'Shakespearean Chartist Hymn Book'. (You will find one of these hymns on p. 90.) Cooper believed that education would make Chartists happier even if it didn't make them richer. He began a Sunday school for adult Chartists. The classes were named after Chartist leaders or dead heroes like William Tell and George Washington. The students were taught to read and write and Cooper lectured on history, geography and poets such as Shakespeare, Milton and Robert Burns.

O'Connor and Cooper and their supporters disliked both *Whigs* and *Tories*. Both parties rejected the Charter completely. Both were supported by people who were rich, or at least had more money than Chartists. Farmers and country landowners supported both parties, but business men in towns supported the Whigs mostly. O'Connor and Cooper disliked Whigs more than Tories. Many working men had helped the Whigs when they had got the 1832 Reform Bill through Parliament, and had then found that the bill did not give working

The Midland Counties'

ILLUMINATOR,

BEING DEVOTED

TO THE INTERESTS

OF THE

WORKING-CLASSES,

Will be found a very advantageous

ADVERTISING MEDIUM,

Especially to those Tradesmen and Shopkeepers whose Establishments are supported chiefly by the Working - Classes. Our Advertising Prices are low ; and favours of this kind will be gratefully received by the Editor.

.*. Our Numbers are now ready every FRIDAY Morning, in Leicester, at Mr. Seal's, Mr. Markham's, and Mr. Windley's,—and may be had, also, on FRIDAY, at Nottingham, of Mr. Sweet; at Loughborough of Mr. Skevington; and on SATURDAY, at Derby, of Mr. Neal; &c. &c. Mr. CLEAVE, 1, Shoe-lane, Fleet-street, LONDON, is our General Agent, and all Booksellers and News-venders in the Country, who receive weekly parcels from him, might order our periodical along with other weekly publications.

An advertisement from the 'Midland Counties' Illuminator

men votes. This is why the Chartists said that the Whigs had 'humbugged' them. Since 1832 Whig governments had created the New Poor Law, persecuted trade unions and prosecuted Chartists. If the Tories had been in power they would have done all these things too, but it was Whig governments that so far Chartists had suffered under.

In 1841 there was a general election. There were only twelve Chartist candidates and none succeeded. This is not surprising since of course the Chartists had very few votes; Cooper says that in Leicester fewer than twenty of the electors were Chartists. In many places the electors, on O'Connor's suggestion,

CHARTIST MEETINGS
FOR THE ENSUING WEEK.

LEICESTER.

THERE will be a General Meeting on Public business To-Night (Saturday, May 15), at Half-past Seven, in the Room at All Saints' Open.

Mr COOPER will preach, at Half-past Six, To-morrow Night (Sunday, May 16) in the same room. Subject :— *The Immortality of the Soul.*

The Collectors are respectfully requested to be punctual in bringing in their books and accounts on Monday night, at Half-past Seven, in order that time may be left for attending to Public business.

The "Chartist Teetotal Section" will meet at Eight o'clock on Tuesday night.

The "Chartist Musical Section" will meet at Eight o'clock on Wednesday night.

WIGSTON.—Mr. Cooper will (if the weather permit) preach in the open air, To-morrow morning (Sunday, May 16,) at Half-past Ten o'clock.

BELGRAVE.—Mr. Cooper will (if the weather permit) preach in the open air, on Sunday Morning, May 23, at Nine o'clock.

THURMASTON.—Mr. Cooper will (if the weather permit) preach in the open air, on Sunday morning, May 23, at Eleven o'clock.

An announcement about Chartist Meetings from the 'Midland Counties' Illuminator'

supported Tories against Whigs. Cooper and O'Connor went over to Nottingham to help the Tory candidate, John Walter, the editor of 'The Times'. They approved of him because he hated the New Poor Law, but Cooper said to Walter, 'Don't have a wrong idea of why you are to have Chartist support. We mean to use your party to cut the throats of the Whigs, and then we mean to cut your throats also.' Walter laughed, 'but he understood that the jest was an earnest one'.

Back in Leicester Cooper came to an arrangement with the Tories. The Tories had no intention of wasting their money by standing for Leicester, where the voters were Whigs, but they did want to make a splash at the 'show of hands'—the cere-mony before the *polling* when party supporters cheered their candidates at the *hustings*. Joseph Phillips, a Leicester banker, offered the Chartists 2*s* 6*d* each if they would put up their hands for a Tory, who would then withdraw. This Cooper agreed to get his followers to do, and in return 'three small linen bags were given me, each containing £10 in silver; and I paid away every coin to the poor ragged men, and wished I had ten times as much to give them'.

Cooper's followers also had a fight with some Whigs at the election, and one gets the feeling when reading Cooper's auto-biography that this was as welcome as the money. One Char-tist flag-bearer drooped his cotton flag near some Whigs, who took insult at this. 'The *gudgeons* caught the bait! They seized the poor little calico flag and tore it to pieces.' The Chartists in return tore up the Whig flags, but these were made of silk and were worth £70!

9 1842: Petition, 'Plug Plot' and Riot

In 1842 the slump returned, worse than ever. Cooper's shop lost business. He began to allow people to have bread 'on tick' and got into debt. He had to close his school 'because the men were too despairing to care about learning to read'. 'What do we care about reading,' said some stocking-weavers to him, 'if we can get nought to eat?' Cooper adds:

'About the same time—I think it was the same week—another poor stockinger rushed into my house, and, throwing himself wildly on a chair, exclaimed, "I wish they would hang me! I have lived on cold potatoes that were given me for two days; and this morning I've eaten a raw potato for sheer hunger! Give me a bit of bread, and a cup of coffee, or I shall drop." I should not like again to see a human face with the look of half insane despair which that poor man's countenance wore.'

Crowds of unemployed stockingers began to beg from door to door, and to march through the streets in huge processions. Many years later Mary Kirby wrote down her memories of life in Leicester during Chartist times; this is what she said about these processions.

'In the Market Place a great crowd of the unemployed used to collect, and with plenty of hooting and shouting (which we could hear as we sat at home) listened to addresses from their leaders; and when the speeches were over, the men would come tramping down Friar Lane, half a dozen or more abreast, and make a great noise, that was intended for singing. The song was all about the Charter and had a refrain of

"Spread—spread the Charter
Spread the Charter through the Land
Let Britons bold and brave join hand and hand!"'

A Leicester Street in 1846. Notice the omnibus

This song was sung to the tune of 'Rule, Britannia'. They also sang hymns from the 'Shakespearean Hymn Book' and the song about O'Connor, 'The Lion of Freedom', which was written by Cooper to celebrate O'Connor's release from prison in August 1841.

> The lion of freedom comes from his den,
> We'll rally around him again and again,
> We'll crown him with laurels our champion to be,
> O'Connor, the patriot of sweet liberty.
>
> The pride of the nation, he's noble and brave
> He's the terror of tyrants, the friend of the slave,
> The bright star of freedom, the noblest of men,
> We'll rally around him again and again.
>
> Though proud daring tyrants his body confined,
> They never could alter his generous mind;

We'll hail our caged lion, now free from his den,
And we'll rally around him again and again.

Who strove for the patriots? was up night and day?
And saved them from falling to tyrants a prey?
It was Feargus O'Connor was diligent then!
We'll rally around him again and again.

Early in 1842 the Poor Law Guardians in Leicester set up a corn mill in the workhouse which was to be turned by hand, by the inmates. The Guardians' refusal to use steam or wind power was deliberate. The mill was planned to deter men from applying to the workhouse. The men hated the mill, and hated the coarse bread they were given even more; they were so badly fed that they had to beg for extra food from the Leicester shops.

One morning some inmates of the workhouse refused to work the hand-mill and barricaded themselves in a room. It took forty-one policemen to get them out. A few days later four inmates did 21s worth of damage to the mill; for this they were all given twenty-one days' hard labour. Their friends quite rightly thought that this sentence was very harsh, and 200 men (many of them Chartists) broke the workhouse windows and threatened to throw the miller in charge of the hand-mill over a railway bridge. They were arrested and at their trial they were defended by Thomas Cooper, who was now a part-time assistant to a local solicitor. In court Cooper bullied witnesses and enjoyed losing his temper. His Chartist supporters were in the gallery, and until the magistrates stopped him Cooper often made political comments in his speeches—calling the New Poor Law, for example, 'the most harsh, inhuman, hellish law ever created'. But despite his efforts the rioters were sent to gaol.

In May O'Connor and his friends presented a new petition

The procession taking the 1842 petition to Parliament. Notice the size of the petition and the children with their hoops

to Parliament. It was signed by 3,317,752 people and had to be taken to the House of Commons by fifty men, each carrying a bundle. With supporters they made a procession two miles long. Like the first petition the second was rejected. Very few M.P.s had a good word to say for the Charter. Most of them thought it was 'utterly incompatible with the very existence of civilisation', that is, they thought that if the Charter were granted it would be impossible to live a civilised life.

By now the slump was at its worst, all over Britain. The 'Manchester Times' said, on 9 July:

'Any man passing through the district and observing the condition of the people, will at once perceive the deep and ravaging distress that prevails, laying industry prostrate, desolating families, and spreading abroad discontent and misery where recently happiness and content were

36

A Radical M.P. presenting the 1842 Chartist petition to the House of Commons

enjoyed. Hungry and half-clothed men and women are stalking through the streets begging for bread.'

A soup kitchen in Manchester was giving 1,000 gallons of soup a day to the poor, many of whom would have starved without it. Nearby, one man wrote 'Stockport to Let' on the door of an empty house. The owners of cotton mills themselves faced bankruptcy. To avoid it they wanted to reduce wages. On Sunday 7 August about 9,000 workers in cotton mills went to a large protest meeting on Mottram Moor near Manchester. The meeting called for the Charter and 'a fair day's wage for a fair day's work'. A strike began in Ashton-under-Lyne and very quickly it spread throughout the cotton area. To force all factories to close, many strikers toured round pulling the plugs from the boilers of the steam engines. For this reason the strike was called the 'Plug Plot'. But there was no plot—just a strike by people who felt that 'life was become a round of helpless drudgery'.

Soldiers at Euston Station, leaving to put down Chartist riots, August 1842

From Lancashire the strike spread to the rest of the North, to Scotland, and the Midlands. By the middle of August many thousands were on strike, including all the Leicester stocking-weavers. On Monday 15 August and the two following days there were mass meetings of the strikers in Leicester Market Place. They said that they would stay on strike till the Charter

Attack on the workhouse at Stockport, August 1842. Notice that the rioters are giving away bread they have looted from the workhouse

was law. They marched round the town singing the Chartist songs and forcing the weavers who were still at work to stop. If they would not, their frames were broken. One old man was badly beaten, his spectacles broken and his face cut, for refusing to stop. Chartists could be brutal.

The Leicester magistrates, seeing the anger of the Chartists and hearing reports of riots from many towns in Britain, were scared. There were fifty policemen in the town, and since they were paid far more than stocking-weavers—18*s* a week—and therefore ate more, they were much fitter and were able to control a small crowd of strikers. But expecting very large crowds of desperate Chartists the magistrates called out the *yeomanry* and recruited 100 special constables.

On Thursday 18 March there were riots and battles with the

police and yeomanry. This is how Daniel Merrick remembered them when he wrote in the 1870s:

'A great crowd of Chartists gathered in the Market Place and a number of policemen, armed with strong *staves*, appeared on the scene and took up a position on the outside of the crowd. Several magistrates, the Mayor and other gentlemen, with a strong guard of policemen, made for the platform, and going up to the chairman, Mr Coulson, peremptorily bade him go and the people to disperse. The vast crowd was in a state of feverish excitement. Amid great uproar and confusion the Mayor read the *Riot Act*. The Chartists adjourned to the Recreation Ground, leaving the Mayor and magistrates in the Market Place. When the meeting was over they again formed the procession, and marched arm in arm up Welford Road. There a fresh surprise awaited them. Mounted cavalry, with drawn swords, were occupying the centre of the road, with police-

Members of the Leicestershire Yeomanry in Chartist times. Drawn by a schoolgirl of the time

men and special constables on either side. Some of them were mounted and armed with cutlasses. When it was seen that the Chartists passed quietly along on either side, the cavalry immediately began to ride pell mell amongst them, and used their swords; the police and constables also drew their staves and struck out indiscriminately, and with great force. Numbers were seriously injured, and one or two, either from fear or violence, died. Many escaped by taking refuge in the entries, but several were made prisoners.'

It is hard to find out the truth about fights and battles. They happen so quickly and people's memories of them are so confused. Merrick sympathised with the Chartists and blamed the soldiers, not the Chartists, for starting the fight. But the police afterwards said that the Chartists began by throwing stones at the horses and this is possible.

One of the arrested men that Merrick mentions was a flag-bearer who was carrying a letter written that morning. The letter was later printed in the 'Leicester Chronicle'. Here it is. If you read it carefully you will see that the Chartists planned to seize food from shops.

Leicester, Aug 18th 1842.

Dear Father,

Spread the Charter through the land. Let Britons bold and brave join hand in hand. I write you these few lines to inform you of my circumstances: my wife is on the point of Death. She has got the Fever, and I am altogether in an unsettled State. I must now inform you of the State of our town, we have had meetings every Night this week consisting of from 3 to 2,000 men, yesterday morning a body of persons came round to our shop and fetched us out; they then commenced to fetch the *cut up hands* and the *wrought hose hands* out, they assembled at Night to the tune of 20,000 men or upwards and swore that by the Ghost of many a murdered Englishman and English woman, they would work no more till the People's Charter becomes the charter of the land, they are assembled this moment in the Market Place, and before the day is over they mean to fetch the Bread and Beef where it is to be had, they are going round now. I am just informed while I am writing that they are stopping all the mills and factories and God speed the plow, you will see that I am working Gloves at William Adams, Burleys Lane, Church Gate, Leicester. I remain your Son and Brother Chartist,

William Corah.

N.B. they are all Chartists here,

please to send this directly to Sam Lintwiters, Ashby Road, Loughborough.

Do you recognise the first two sentences of this letter? Do you think that the Leicester magistrates were right to be worried? There was in fact more trouble on Friday 19 August. In the morning about 500 strikers gathered at the end of Humberstone Gate to march to Loughborough. They were soon overtaken by the Chief Constable with some police and yeomanry. The strikers, armed with iron bars, poles and walking sticks, took up position on top of Mowmaker Hill. But when the yeomanry charged them they fled. This was the 'battle of Mowmaker Hill'. Ten years after a Leicester poet treated the whole affair as a joke, in 'The Battle of Mowmaker Hill: an heroic-comic poem', but at the time it did not seem funny. The magistrates of Leicester were scared, and as a result they acted cruelly. William Jones, a Chartist from Liverpool, was arrested for making a speech which the police called *inflammatory*; that is, likely to make people burn with rage and therefore riot again. His most inflammatory words were calling the police 'blue vampires', the 'unboiled blue', and predicting that 'when the day of boiling comes, Woe to the unboiled'. For this he got six months in gaol.

10 Thomas Cooper in Manchester

Reading the Riot Act in Manchester, August 1842

Cooper was not in Leicester during the troubles of August 1842. Another Chartist Convention had been arranged some time before, to take place in Manchester; by a coincidence the strikes broke out just before it met. Cooper planned to go to Manchester, and to travel by way of Staffordshire, so that he could collect money owing to him for his Chartist newspapers. Setting out on 9 August, he spoke at a large meeting in Birmingham and to striking coalminers in the Black Country. At Stafford he noticed policemen taking notes of his speech, so he quickly turned it into a sarcastic defence of the things the

Chartists disliked most. As he later wrote to his followers in Leicester:

'I showed how excellent it was to have a "sweet little silver-voiced lady", and pay one million and a quarter yearly to support her. I demonstrated that working men would weep their eyes sore if Adelaide were to be deprived of her £100,000 a year.' [Adelaide was the widow of king William IV; the capital of South Australia was named after her.] 'I denounced any ragged shoemaker [Stafford, you know, my brave Shakespeareans, is a famous shoe-making town] as a stupid fellow, if he dared to talk about his aged grandmother being in a *bastille*, and starving on "*skilly*", while Adelaide had three palaces to live in.'

Who was the 'sweet little silver-voiced lady'?

On Sunday 14 August he was in Hanley, in the Potteries, just as the Chartist troubles were starting, and he addressed a meeting in the evening. As was natural for someone who had

been a Methodist *lay preacher* Cooper took as the motto for his speech the sixth commandment, 'Thou shalt not kill'. 'I declared that all who helped to maintain the system of labour which reduced poor stockingers to the starvation I had seen in Leicester were breaking the commandment, "Thou shalt do no murder".' For some time Cooper went on in the same way, and made his audience angry. To arouse men in this way so that they might cause a riot was, and is still, against the law. Cooper thought that he was keeping within the law by adding, right at the end of his speech, a warning to his audience that they had to forgive their enemies. But this was not enough— in any case his hearers took no notice of the warning—and later Cooper was to pay heavily for this speech and others like it.

On Monday 15 August Cooper spoke to another meeting of about 10,000 and urged them to strike until the Charter was law. All hands were raised in agreement, says Cooper. The crowd then marched to Longton, followed by two fearful magistrates on horseback and some soldiers marching with fixed bayonets. Expecting trouble the shopkeepers shut up their shops and drove away. Hanley became a 'human desert'. The local Chartists, mostly coalminers, burned down

Staffordshire miners in the 1840s

the houses of men they especially hated—magistrates and mine managers. Chartists and soldiers fought in the streets, and when some Chartists tried to unhorse the cavalry they opened fire and one Chartist was killed.

Cooper wrote to his supporters in Leicester telling them that they should gather all Chartists together in the Market Place and get them to strike until the Charter was law. He dared not trust this letter to the post; Chartists' letters were sometimes opened and in any case he wanted the letter to arrive very quickly. So he paid a local Chartist 5s to carry it to Leicester; he walked all night and reached Leicester early in the morning. Meanwhile, Cooper had left the Potteries in the evening of 15 August to travel to Manchester. Fearing arrest, he borrowed a hat and greatcoat from the landlord of the 'George and Dragon' and in this disguise walked to Crewe, where he caught the train to Manchester.

The Chartists at the Convention could not decide what to do. They had not planned the strikes, which took them by surprise. Some men wanted the strikes to develop into a full-scale revolution; Cooper was one of them, and he 'told them that the spread of the strikes would and must be followed by a general outbreak. The authorities would try to quell it; but the Chartists must resist them. There was nothing now but a physical force struggle to be looked for. The Chartists must get the people out to fight; and they would be irresistible if they were united.'

Some men advised caution. O'Connor, no longer hoping as he had in 1839 to bluff the government into surrender by making threats of violence that he did not really intend to back up, argued with Cooper that all talk of the use of force was wrong. Another Chartist, Otley, said to Cooper:

'How can you expect poor starving weavers to fight? and what have they to fight with? Have you calculated that if we try to form battalions for fighting, the people will need

46

food and clothing—they will need arms and powder and shot? They would, very likely, have to camp in the fields. How can you expect poor weavers to do that?'

Cooper and his friends won the debate. The Convention published a fiery *manifesto* calling for a general strike throughout Britain till the Charter was law; it was expected that the strike would develop into a violent struggle. The manifesto ended with a clear call for the use of force. 'Strengthen our hands at this crisis; support your leaders; rally round our sacred cause; and leave the decision to the God of Justice and of battle.'

The strike failed. The government and the employers stood firm and by the end of the month all the strikers, facing starvation if they stayed out any longer, were back at work. By October most of the Chartist leaders were in prison for their inflammatory language. Cooper was arrested on his return to Leicester, for his speeches at Hanley. His trial was eventually fixed for March 1843 and meanwhile he was allowed out on bail. Back in Leicester for a few months, Cooper found his following as large as ever, but he was badly in debt—to the printer of his newspapers, and to a baker on account of the bread he had given away to the poor. He tried to make some money by staging 'Hamlet' in the Amphitheatre, playing the Prince of Denmark himself, of course. But the other actors had to be paid, and, though Cooper says that the theatre was full on both evenings (which is probably an exaggeration), he made no money.

At his trial Cooper defended himself, speaking for ten hours, but was convicted of sedition and sent to prison for two years. As he enters Stafford gaol he passes out of the Chartist story almost entirely—but you may read about what happened to him on p. 73.

11   The Chartist Land Plan

After 1842 life was better for some years in Leicester and elsewhere; men were still poor, but only a few were still starving.
There were no longer huge Chartist meetings, processions and
riots. Yet as O'Connor said in 1844: 'Chartism is not dead,
but sleeping'.

In these years O'Connor was busy with his land plan, to
settle thousands of Chartists from towns on *smallholdings* in the
countryside, where they would earn their living as farmers.
He explained his plan in several books, many speeches, and
many articles in the 'Northern Star'. If thousands of working
men settled on the land there would be fewer men competing
for industrial jobs. Unemployment would go down and the
wages of the men who stayed in industry would go up. (One
of the reasons why wages were so low in Leicester was that
there were too many stocking-weavers.) In the country the
settlers would be richer, and they would not be under the
control of a factory boss, or of machinery, 'which ought to be
man's slave, and has become man's master'. He put it like this
to the Chartists: 'You are, in a word, a poor, beggarly, lousy
set of devils! Without house or home, or bread, or clothes, or
fuel, begging the means of subsistence, and thankful to him
who will coin your sweat into gold! Now mark what you might
be—comfortable, independent, happy.'

O'Connor founded the Chartist Co-operative Land Society
in 1845. It was later renamed the National Land Company.
Chartists were invited to buy shares in the company for £1. 6s
each; they could pay for them in instalments of as little as
one shilling. The money paid in would be used to buy land
which would be split up into smallholdings of two, three or
four acres. The shareholders would then ballot for the plots.

Two shares would entitle their holder to try for a two-acre plot, three shares a three-acre plot, and four shares a four-acre plot. Each settler would also get a cottage; schools, libraries and hospitals would be built for each Chartist colony. The settlers would have *leases* of their plots for ever, but they would pay a rent of £1 5s an acre, which would help to buy more land. In this way, O'Connor predicted, all the shareholders would get plots in a few years. 'I would make a paradise of England in less than FIVE YEARS.'

The settlers would support themselves by cultivating land by use of a spade; with one they could grow enough to keep themselves very comfortably. O'Connor had a wild faith in the power of the spade, compared with that of the plough. Constant digging enriched the soil, but ploughing did not; a lot of manure was not necessary. 'One good digging is worth three ploughings. The best manure is that found in the arms of a man.' He mentioned many times the wonders he had achieved as a farmer in Ireland by means of spade cultivation; like many of his stories, they are unconvincing. He argued that four acres, properly dug, would produce 371,712 pounds of potatoes, or in different crops would feed a man and six members of his family, provide more than enough wool and linen to clothe them, and still leave enough produce over to fetch £124. 2s a year.

Apparently exact details made O'Connor's yarns seem true and acceptable; he took in many Chartists who hungered for a better and healthier life but had little knowledge of what farming was like. Very quickly there were about 300 branches of the land company with 70,000 subscribers. They were in all parts of the country, and in particular in the large towns that people would naturally want to get out of and where there had been most Chartists anyway. In Leicester there were three branches of the land company; one met every Monday evening at seven o'clock at 17 Archdeacon Lane; lists of the

Leicester subscribers were printed regularly in the 'Northern Star'.

The first estate, of 102 acres at Heronsgate near Watford in Hertfordshire, was bought for £2,344 in March 1846. It was called O'Connorville. Allotments were marked out and cottages built. Those on the three or four-acre plots had two storeys, with two or three bedrooms, a kitchen and a parlour. The two-acre plots had bungalows with one large living-room and kitchen, and two bedrooms. All had farm outbuildings. At the other four Chartist settlements only bungalows were built, whatever the acreage of the plots. Sometimes they were made of local stone, sometimes of brick, but in size and shape the bungalows were always the same. They were well built, with stone floors and slate roofs, and were much larger than the two-roomed cabins that many farm labourers lived in the

A Chartist bungalow at Dodford. Its appearance has scarcely altered since 1848

1840s. O'Connor was very proud of his cottages, and was delighted to watch the carpenters and bricklayers busy at work on them.

In Manchester on 10 April 1846 a ballot was held to choose

the first thirty-five settlers at O'Connorville; thirteen got four acres, five three acres and seventeen two acres. Everything was going well. In July the carpenters and bricklayers at O'Connorville played a cricket match, which was duly reported in the 'Northern Star'. The bricklayers won by twenty-eight runs. Afterwards the players drank milk, praised by O'Connor as 'the most wholesome, the most nutritious, and the most grateful beverage', though in fact he was becoming increasingly fond of brandy himself. (No public houses were to be permitted at the land colonies, but one with a Chartist name, the 'Land of Liberty', was soon opened at O'Connorville. It still exists. The public house at Snig's End, the 'Prince

The 'Prince of Wales', Snig's End: once the Chartist school. The boys' wing is on the left, the girls' on the right, the schoolmaster's house in the middle

WORKING MEN'S COLLEGE / IBR

of Wales', was built as the school for the settlement by the land company.)

Between the plots roads were built and the men lucky in the ballot named them after the towns they were from—Bradford Road, Halifax Road, Nottingham Road and Stockport Road. In August a special celebration of the plan's start was held at O'Connorville. A procession of carriages and coaches left Hyde Park Corner at seven a.m. and arrived at O'Connorville at noon. There were refreshments and dancing for the 12,000 who attended from all parts of Britain. O'Connor made a speech, while waving a huge cabbage: 'I wish to see the cottage the castle of the freeman, instead of the den of the slave.' A young Chartist, Ernest Jones, wrote a poem for the occasion:

> 'In crowded town the poor mechanic wakes,
> But why today, at twilight's early prime,
> When moon's grey finger points the march of time,
> Why starts he upwards with a joyous strength
> To face the long day slavery's cheerless length?
> Has freedom whispered in his wistful ear,
> "Courage, poor slave! deliverance is near!?"
> Oh! she has breathed a summons sweeter still:
> "Come! take your *guerdon* at O'Connorville!"'

The settlers moved into O'Connorville on May Day 1847.

Soon three more estates were bought and divided in the same way: Lowbands and Snig's End near Gloucester and Minster Lovell near Witney in Oxfordshire; this one was called Charterville. In all about 250 shareholders were lucky in the ballot. Who were they? It is not possible now to find out the names and jobs of all of them, but we do know that while a few had been farm labourers most were from towns. Five were stocking-weavers from Leicester; one of these, John Hawksworth, came by cart to Snig's End, where his grand-

O'Connor Villa, Snig's End. Another Chartist cottage. O'Connor is thought to have lived here for a time early in 1848

daughter still lives. Another stocking-weaver went to Low-bands, where a fairly full list has been made of the jobs the settlers had had. There were two factory foremen, a cotton spinner, a shoemaker, a tallow chandler, two cabinetmakers, a lace weaver, a tailor, two brass founders from Birmingham, and a furrier, Wolf Moss, who had been born in Prussia. One would like to know what had brought him to England and made him a Chartist.

Twenty-three of the successful balloters sold their rights to smallholdings to other subscribers; one man got £90 for a winning ticket. The sellers did better out of the land plan than anyone else. Unfortunately it was never really successful, and a good deal of the blame was O'Connor's. He was an intelligent, kindhearted man with a great sympathy for poor people. He was also reckless and careless. He spoke without thinking and published extravagant plans which looked good on paper but which were not practical. Skilled farmers would have found it hard to make a good living from a few acres, even on ideal land with markets nearby for their produce. Many of the settlers had had gardens but growing radishes and flowers as a hobby is very different from earning one's living from the soil. Encouraged by O'Connor they came with exaggerated ideas of the amount they could easily grow. As the 'Edinburgh Review' put it:

'Every acre was to yield on an average such crops as no acre ever did yield except under the rarest combinations of favouring climate, consummate skill, and unlimited manure—and then only occasionally. Every cow was to live for ever, was to give more milk than any save the most exceptional cow ever gave before, and was never to be dry. Every pig was to be a prize one, every goose to be a swan.'

O'Connor wrote that it was unnecessary to feed cows on grass; he recommended cabbages and swedes. One expert, J. R. Revans, pointed out that cabbages would make the cows diarrhoetic and swedes would give the milk 'a nauseous flavour'.

Revans found the land at all four settlements poor and the allotments too small to provide a living by themselves. O'Connor argued that the owners of very small farms in the Channel Islands managed to live very well; Revans pointed out that the farmers also worked as fishermen on the Newfoundland fisheries. Revans found the crops at O'Connorville not as good as those on farms nearby. The settlers were inexperienced and had to hire local farm labourers to work for them. Ploughs had to be borrowed from friendly farmers. Nine of the settlers left after a few months because their wives could not make butter or bake bread.

At Snig's End a farmer said of the settlers, 'These poor

people are expected to get off an acre as much as I could get off 100'. They could not make a living growing potatoes and started to make gloves. This business failed too. At Lowbands the settlers used special two-pronged forks to work the heavy clay soil but it was 'out of heart'. Worst off were the settlers at Charterville, where one Chartist knew so little that he thrashed a pig for squealing! The settlement was on top of a hill where high winds blew and the soil was thin. The wife of one of the settlers came from Minster Lovell, sheltered in the valley below, and she thought that going to live in Charterville was like going into exile. It was 'a terrible place to bring anyone to'. Local people said that they would take allotments there only if they had no rent to pay and other jobs to live on.

The Charterville land was *mortgaged* by O'Connor to raise money to buy more estates; when he was no longer able to pay the interest on the loan the moneylenders evicted all except two of the tenants in November 1850. The two that were left became farm labourers.

The greatest fault in the running of the scheme was in fact the way in which the money was muddled. O'Connor was disgracefully careless with his own money and other people's. The subscribers paid about £100,000 into the company. About £45,000 were spent on buying the land and a lot more on buildings. But no proper accounts were kept and the offices were in great confusion. This was shown in a report of the *Select Committee* of the House of Commons that enquired fully into the scheme in 1848. It showed that O'Connor had not been dishonest; he had in fact lost £3,000 of his own money in the plan. It also showed that O'Connor's notion of settling all the subscribers in five years was nonsense; one expert witness pointed out that it would have taken 150 years at the plan's rate of progress. Most of the other Chartist leaders—Lovett, O'Brien, Cooper—had attacked the plan from the start. O'Brien pointed out that if O'Connor had bought land at the rate needed to settle the subscribers quickly the price of land would have gone up and the scheme would have been wrecked anyway.

The report of the Select Committee destroyed confidence in O'Connor and his scheme and subscriptions petered out. There was one last settlement, at Great Dodford near Bromsgrove in Worcestershire. Here thirty-six settlers moved into four-acre plots in the summer of 1849. The Select Committee had disapproved of the ballot method and at Dodford the plots went to subscribers who could put down large sums of money, ranging between £55 and £150. No stocking-weaver could afford this and there were none at Dodford. The settlers included a pawnbroker, a plumber, a carpenter, a shoemaker, a pensioner of the *East India Company*, a glassmaker, a grocer, a stone-miner, a hatter, a brickmaker, and three stonemasons.

For some time O'Connor hoped to be able to start more settlements and in August 1850 he declared in the 'Northern Star' that he planned to go on a lecture tour 'to propound the means by which every industrious man may be freed from the rasp of the bloodsucker by the application of free labour to the cultivation of HIS OWN LAND!' He had no success. In August 1851 the National Land Company was ended by Act of Parliament. The settlers could stay on if they could afford rent but in fact by 1851 three-quarters of the settlers in the original four colonies had already left. Some settlers stayed on and used their plots to add to their earnings in other jobs—usually as farm labourers. Dodford was the only colony where the settlers managed to make most of their living from their plots alone. The soil was very heavy and the O'Connor plan of growing wheat, potatoes and vegetables was as unprofitable there as elsewhere. But one settler, John Wallace, had been gardener to the Earl of Plymouth at Tardebigge a few miles away. He realised that strawberries could be grown, if the ground was properly manured, and that they could be sold in

The Priory, Dodford: O'Connor's home in the summer of 1848

Birmingham nearby. At his suggestion the settlers turned their plots over to growing 'Dodford strawberries', famous in the Midlands until about forty years ago for their size and sweetness. At the Dodford Strawberry Wake, held on the second Sunday in July every year until 1922, merchants came to taste and buy the crop. The settlers grew vegetables and kept chickens and often added to their income by making nails at home.

In 1872 thirteen of the original settler families were still in Dodford—a higher proportion than in any of the other colonies—and some were still there at the end of the century. They continued to be Radicals, and at elections they marched under a banner that had embroidered on it the slogan 'Dodford Independent Electors. Ready? Yes, always ready'. The local vicar, a Conservative, called them 'rag, tag and bobtail'.

After the First World War strawberries became less profitable, for several reasons. The smallholders began to work in Midlands factories, as they still do. Now some of the plots are overgrown, some are orchards, some poultry-runs or gardens, some part of nearby farms; one is covered with caravans and another is a chicken 'factory farm'. The very narrow lanes and the cottages, now modernised, look very much as they did in Chartist days, except for the television aerials. Three of the other settlements look very much like Dodford. O'Connorville is now part of a rich suburb of London; the plots are gardens and many of the cottages have been enlarged. But the narrow roads are still there, with the names given them by the first settlers in July 1846, and shaded by the trees they planted.

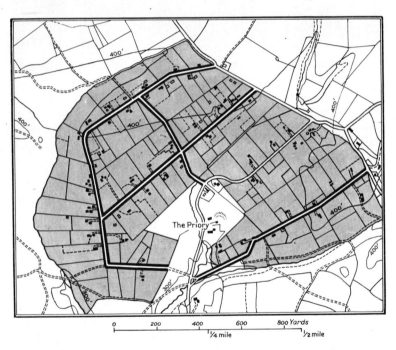

Dodford today: the area of the Chartist Colony is shaded on the map, and the lanes specially built for it are marked in black. The boundaries of many of the Chartist plots may still be seen on the map, though some of the plots have been split up and others have been added together. The size and shape of the plots should be compared with those of the ordinary fields in the top right-hand corner of the map. Most of the buildings marked are Chartist cottages

12 1848: The Third Petition

The slump returned in 1847. In Leicester there were so many men unemployed that, as in previous years, despite the New Poor Law they could not all be crammed into the workhouse. So they were given outdoor relief and made to break stones all day. For this they were given a few pence a day. Let Daniel Merrick once again tell us what life was like in Leicester.

‘It was now winter, and the stoneyards were situated by the side of the canal. The cold air from the water shrivelled the men up until some looked as though they had deserted from a graveyard. The morning scene in these stoneyards

Breaking stone in a workhouse

E

would have been a good subject for a picture. Some of the men went to the yards with faces unwashed and unshaven, with scarves of various colours round their necks. Some wore pieces of flannel torn off an old petticoat and others had their wives' shawls tied round their mouths and chins, while others had overcoats, or what had once been over-coats. Some were almost destitute, having nothing to cover them except rags.'

Chartism revived. This time it was encouraged by the revolutions on the continent of Europe, where almost every country had one in 1848. One of the earliest was in France, and this helped to cause the others and heartened the Chartists. A Chartist described the effect on a meeting of Chartists and European revolutionaries of the news that the king of France had fled and a republic set up in France:

'The effect was electrical. Frenchmen, Germans, Poles, Magyars sprang to their feet, embraced and shouted in the wildest enthusiasm. Snatches of *oratory* were delivered in excited tones, and flags were taken from the walls, to be waved exultantly, amidst cries of "Vive la République!". Then the doors were opened, and the whole assembly, with linked arms and colours flying, marched to the meeting place of the Westminster Chartists in Dean Street, Soho. Great was the clinking of glasses that night in and around Soho and Leicester Square.'

In Glasgow thousands of unemployed workers rioted and plundered shops, crying 'Vive la République!' Harney, now editor of the 'Northern Star', wrote, under the pen name of 'L'Ami du Peuple' (Friend of the People): 'The French, with three days' work, have obtained the Charter and something more'. In Leicester a large meeting in the Amphitheatre sent its congratulations to the French Republic.

A third petition and another National Convention were decided on. The Leicester Chartists elected as their delegate a framework-knitter called George Buckby. When he was about to set off for London a huge meeting was held in his honour. About 8,000 Chartists gathered in the Market Place, and then marched in procession to take Buckby to the station. At the head marched men carrying the Leicester section of the petition, with 42,884 signatures covering 143 yards of paper.

The forty-seven delegates to the Convention decided that

The Chartist Convention, 1848

there would be a Chartist meeting on Kennington Common on 10 April. From there a procession would take the petition to Westminster. O'Connor certainly wanted this to be a peaceful demonstration and said that when he was asked what the Chartists intended to do on 10 April, he would reply that 'not one pane of glass, nor one pennyworth of property, would be injured'. Other delegates would have welcomed a chance to turn the procession into something more violent. They were excited by the success of the revolutions on the continent. They naturally expected this petition to be rejected like the others, and they looked forward to a revolution in England in 1848. Some Chartists were secretly planning armed uprisings to take place in the summer.

The government knew, or guessed at, these plans, and was determined to take no chances on 10 April or afterwards. Since 1839 Britain had been covered by two networks—railways and telegraph wires—which the government was now

London policemen ready for trouble, April 1848

able to use against any attempt at revolution. Soldiers were placed at a few carefully chosen towns, ready to move by train at an hour's notice. The army, wrote Harney, was 'seated like a spider in the centre of its web, on the diverging lines of iron road'. Government information could be quickly sent by telegraph—and Chartists were to be unable to use the system. Only those with passes signed by the Home Secretary were to get near the transmitting keys.

Careful preparations were made in London. The procession was banned, and to prevent any mass crossing of the Thames (Kennington Common is south of the river), the bridges were heavily guarded by infantry and cavalry. Other soldiers were placed, nearly out of sight so as not to provoke trouble, round Kennington Common itself and near the Bank of England.

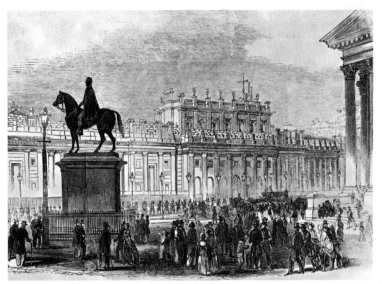

Guarding the Bank of England, 1848. Notice the special constables, and the sandbags round the roof

Thirty heavy field guns were in the Tower and steamers were hired to take them up river to bombard crowds threatening the bridges. 150,000 special constables were recruited. (They included Napoleon's great-nephew, soon to leave London and become the Emperor Napoleon III.) *Civil servants* were armed, and government offices and the Bank of England defended by sandbag parapets and timber barricades, pierced with loopholes for rifle fire.

63

The early morning of 10 April was fine and warm as the Chartist processions drew near Kennington Common from

The Chartist procession to Kennington Common

all over London. Many thousands of men marched about in the sunshine under flags and banners. O'Connor afterwards claimed that 500,000 men were present. The Prime Minister told the Queen 15,000. He was nearer the truth. The Chartist leaders were the last to arrive, in a wagon behind another carrying the huge bulk of the petition and decorated with red, green and white tricolour flags.

O'Connor was worried and ill. He had hardly slept for six nights and there was a pain in his chest which might have been caused by nervousness. He could be very brave in a fight but underneath his blustering and boasting he was often very timid, especially as he grew older and more and more unbalanced mentally. As his wagon started to cross Kennington Common a police inspector stopped it and asked him to come to meet Colonel Mayne, the Metropolitan Police Commis-

The Kennington Common Meeting

sioner. O'Connor agreed. As they left the common the crowd yelled 'They have got him!' and surged forward. This was the nearest the day got to violence. Gradually the rush died down and the crowd waited.

O'Connor met Mayne in a public house nearby. Mayne noticed that O'Connor looked pale and frightened. Mayne told him that the procession would not be allowed to cross the river. O'Connor did not argue. He thanked Mayne as warmly as though he had done him a favour, and much to the colonel's astonishment, insisted on shaking him by the hand. Back on the common O'Connor begged the crowd to disperse. 'I would go down on my knees to beseech you—do not now destroy the cause I have struggled for all my life.' The crowd did disperse. The petition was placed in three cabs. O'Connor entered another and then went with the petition to the House of Commons. As he left the sun was covered with clouds and drenching rain began, soaking the Chartists gloomily marching home.

A GREAT DEMONSTRATION.

Mob-Orator. "TELL ME, MINION! IS IT THE INTENTION OF YOUR PROUD MASTERS AT ALL HAZARDS TO PREVENT OUR DEMONSTRATION !"
Magistrate (blandly). "YES, SIR."
Mob-Orator. "THEN KNOW, OH MYRMIDON OF THE BRUTAL WHIGS, THAT I SHALL GO HOME TO MY TEA, AND ADVISE MY COMRADES TO DO THE SAME !"

'Punch's' view of O'Connor's surrender at Kennington Common. A very bad drawing of O'Connor

O'Connor had boasted that the petition had 5,706,000 signatures. When it was examined in the House of Commons it was found to have only 1,975,000, and these included many names like 'Queen Victoria', 'Duke of Wellington', 'Mr Punch' and 'No cheese'; these were not people likely to sign a Chartist petition. Many petitions to the House of Commons had *fictitious* signatures, and O'Connor could have argued that one with over 1,000,000 genuine ones was too important to be ignored. Instead, he made himself ridiculous by challenging one critical M.P. to a duel. He was arrested and forced to apologise to the House of Commons.

Throughout the summer of 1848 the Chartists remained

'Punch's' comment on the strange signatures to the 1848 petition. Many names were fictitious like 'Cheeks the Marine': also, the names of the Conservative politicians, like the Duke of Wellington and Colonel Sibthorp, were forged. You will find nine Wellingtons in this cartoon, and Queen Victoria too, since her signature also appeared in the petition!

active, and nowhere more than in Leicester. In the spring the pauper stonebreakers began to complain that the relief they were given was too small. They begged for extra amounts from shopkeepers and threatened to beat up those who would not give. Sometimes they took goods by force. Early in May the Guardians increased the relief payments to 5s 10d a week for six days' work, but they also ordered the stonebreaking to start at six a.m. instead of eight a.m. The new regulations were to start on Monday 15 May, but on that day all the men agreed not to turn up till eight a.m. They then found the yard gates closed. The men marched in procession through the streets, shouting Chartist slogans and singing Chartist songs. They threw stones at two magistrates who argued with them. In the evening they broke the windows of the houses of two leading Guardians, and made a disturbance until the Mayor arrived at eleven p.m. with a strong force of policemen. The Riot Act was read, but instead of leaving, the crowd began to stone the police. Some army pensioners, who this year had been recruited as special constables, then cleared the rioters with bayonets.

The Bastille Riots (as they were called) lasted for three more days. Garrisons of army pensioners and special constables were placed on buildings like the Town Hall and the workhouse. The town was divided into six areas, each patrolled at night by police commanded by a magistrate. On Thursday a mob surrounded the Bell Hotel and attacked the yeomanry inside; one cavalryman who was riding into the courtyard was pulled from his horse. The same night some Chartists threw stones at the police from houses in Wharf Street. The police broke down the doors and the specials used their truncheons viciously on anyone they found inside. The riots ended when some soldiers from an infantry regiment were brought to the town.

One of the Leicester Chartists, John Markham, protested against the brutality of the police, and a committee was set up by the Chartists to collect evidence on the matter. Unfortunately the committee did very little, but it is interesting because a young Leicester man called Thomas Cook, the first travel agent, served on it.

There was worse trouble in other towns; in Bradford, for example, 2,000 Chartists at the end of May defeated a larger number of police and had to be put down by two companies of infantry, two troops of *dragoons*, the West Yorkshire Yeomanry Cavalry and the Yorkshire *Hussars*. 'The Times' said, 'Let us do the Chartists justice. If fighting with pluck against special constables and the police could make a revolution, those who fought at Bradford ought to have succeeded.'

Meanwhile, some Chartists were planning a large-scale British revolution. We cannot know now exactly who was involved or how wide the plans were. Plots are not written about or reported in newspapers. We do know that in many parts of the country rifles, cartridges, fireballs and *grenades* had been stored. In London we hear of an odd chemical which when mixed with water was to set the capital alight. Nobody knows what this might have been. Irishmen in Liverpool, Manchester, Bolton and other Lancashire towns were plotting with Chartists the overthrow of the hated British government. In Leicestershire there are stories of Chartists storing arms and drilling in the countryside. In June a Leicester Chartist called George Bown published a pamphlet called 'Physical Force', in which his 'sober, earnest, and deliberate advice' to Chartists was 'GET ARMS', though he tried to keep within the law by adding 'I by no means advise their use'. The 'Sheffield Independent' said on 29 April that *pike* blades were being carried through the streets of Barnsley 'as openly as *cutlers* in Sheffield carry their work through the streets. It is quite amusing to hear the children quarrel among themselves as to the quality of their fathers' pikes, and to see them sketch the shape of them on the causeway.'

A rising was planned for 15 August to take place in London, Lancashire and perhaps elsewhere. The London revolutionaries numbered about 1,200 and were organised in 'brigades' and 'divisions', each with a definite task to undertake in the rising. Certain buildings and streets were to be seized at a fixed hour and then barricaded. The Lancashire rising was to take place at the same time. The plots were known to the police, who had planted spies among the plotters. The 'leader' of the 'Wat Tyler Brigade' in Greenwich said afterwards, 'I was not a Chartist, but merely joined them for the purpose of collecting information. I wished to *ingratiate* myself with these people that I might betray them.' There was a police spy among the Leicestershire Chartists too. The spies gave the police plenty of advance warning and there were mass arrests in London and Lancashire. One group of plotters was arrested at the 'Orange Tree' public house in Bloomsbury when they were making their final plans. More than 100 Irishmen at Seven Dials (in central London) and some more armed men near Westminster had already gathered for the rising when the police arrived. Troops had to be used only once, at Ashton-under-Lyne, where the revolutionaries rose early and held the town for a day. By the end of the year the plot leaders were on their way to Australia; they had been tried and sentenced to be transported to a penal colony.

These failures followed the flop in April and came at the same time as the report of the Select Committee on the Chartist Land Company, which showed how foolish the land plan was and how badly it had been managed. As was natural when they were bitterly disappointed, the Chartist leaders were quarrelling with each other. O'Connor took no part in the plots. He and the revolutionaries were split, but other men who agreed with him on this question, like Bronterre O'Brien, despised him for being a coward at Kennington in April and for the failure of his land plan. Now, one Leicestershire Chartist wrote, 'the end was coming. The arrest of so many of the leaders, the severe measures of the government, the feeling that there was no great leader left able to lead the people to victory, were all tending to *demoralise* the party.' At the end of October Harney wrote in the 'Northern Star': 'Popular indifference was never more clearly shown than at this very time. Chartist organisation has become the merest name—the very shadow of a shade.'

13 What Happened to Feargus O'Connor

Fewer and fewer people listened to O'Connor. The circulation of the 'Northern Star' fell from the peak of the 21,000 copies sold of the issue for 15 April 1848, describing the Kennington Common meeting, to fewer than 5,000 copies a week two years later. His health was breaking down and he was going mad. Despite his great size and strength he was often ill in the Chartist years. He nearly died in 1839, suffered badly from rheumatism in prison, and was ill again in 1848. He ruined his health by working furiously for Chartism—always travelling, speaking or writing, hardly ever resting and sleeping for only a few hours a night. By the end of the 1840s his red hair had turned white and his face was thin and lined. He made things worse by turning to strong drink for support. By 1852 he was drinking fifteen glasses of brandy a day.

By 1852 he was insane. Justin McCarthy, for many years an M.P., later described his seeing O'Connor about this time
'sauntering through Covent Garden market, with rolling, restless *gait*; his eyes gleaming with the peculiar, quick, shallow, ever-changing glitter of madness. The poor fellow rambled from fruit-stall to fruit-stall, talking all the while to himself, sometimes taking up a fruit as if he meant to buy it, and then putting it down with a vacant laugh and walking on. It was a pitiable spectacle.'

In 1847 O'Connor had been elected M.P. for Nottingham. In the House of Commons he mimicked the Speaker, slapped Lord Palmerston on the back just as he was about to speak, and punched two members during debates. The *Sergeant-at-Arms* arrested him and he was sent to an asylum at Chiswick. He died in 1855, penniless. His money had been squandered,

Statue of O'Connor in Nottingham

for his funeral at Kensal Green cemetery. In heavy rain 30,000 or 40,000 people attended it and a long procession of working people, following his coffin, carried banners inscribed 'He died for us'.

14 What Happened to Thomas Cooper

We left Thomas Cooper in Stafford gaol in 1843. He was given only gruel, coarse bread, and potatoes, to eat. His cast iron bedstead had no proper mattress and no pillow. Cooper blew up the inflatable rubber pillow he had brought with him but was still uncomfortable. Most of all he resented not being given pens, paper and his books; he wanted to study and write. Cooper showed his toughness of character by making the prison officers' lives miserable till he got what he wanted. 'I was ever knocking at the door, or shattering the windows, or asking for the surgeon or governor, or troubling them in one way or another.' He attended chapel and disturbed the service by grabbing hold of the chaplain and demanding that he should help him. At last a fellow prisoner smuggled in pen and paper to him and Cooper wrote to Thomas Slingsby Duncombe, an M.P. who sympathised with the Chartists and who raised his case in Parliament. Cooper now got better food and furniture, his books, and permission to write. He wrote 'The *Purgatory* of Suicides', a very long poem about the struggle for freedom through the ages. The first verse gives the message of the book:

'Slaves, toil no more! Why delve, and moil, and pine,
To glut the tyrant forgers of your chain?
Slaves, toil no more! Up, from the midnight mine,
Summon your *swarthy* thousands to the plain;
Beneath the bright sun marshalled, swell the strain
Of liberty; and while the lordlings view
Your banded hosts, with stricken heart and brain,
Shout, as one man,—"Toil we no more renew,
Until the Many cease their slavery to the Few!"'

Cooper left prison convinced that violence could not help Chartism and that the land plan of his former idol, O'Connor, was nonsense. In his quarrelsome way he quite wrongly accused O'Connor of stealing the subscribers' money and he was expelled from the 1846 Chartist Convention. He left the movement, playing no part in 1848.

He now earned his living by writing and lecturing. His poem, which seems unreadable now, was admired by many then, including Charles Dickens and William Wordsworth. It was followed by volumes of short stories and three novels, of which the best is probably 'Captain Cobbler: a Story of the Reign of Henry VIII'. His ability as a speaker and his knowledge of so many subjects made it possible for him to tour Britain and Ireland lecturing on the lives of almost every famous man you will find mentioned in your history textbooks, from William Tell to Beau Brummel, and on topics as different as Negro Slavery and Gulliver's Travels.

Since 1841 Cooper had not believed in Christianity, but in 1856 he became reconverted to it, very suddenly in the middle of a lecture. He could no longer speak in public; he was too tongue-tied. For eight years he and his wife wandered throughout England, preaching and very poor. In old age he settled, wrote more stories, another long poem, 'The Paradise of Martyrs', his autobiography, and lastly 'Thoughts at Fourscore'. This shows Cooper as a grumpy, dissatisfied old man. Working men, he says, no longer wanted to educate themselves as he had done sixty years before. They were more interested in playing football or watching it. (The Football Association had been founded in 1863.) What Cooper forgot was that when he was young only a few men had been as interested as he in learning Greek and reading Shakespeare. Cooper had always been an exceptional man, in brain, energy, and bad temper—and also in ability to work furiously for the Chartist stocking-weavers who had followed him.

15 What Happened to the Chartists after 1848

Many Chartists sought a better life overseas after 1848. Some fought with Garibaldi's armies in Italy. One, Allen Pinkerton, was the head of Lincoln's secret service in the American Civil War and then founded the first private detective agency. Another, M. M. Trumbull, was a general in the Northern army. There were Chartists in the Ballarat gold rush in the 1850s; they formed the Ballarat Reform League of 1854 which put forward the Chartist programme on behalf of the working men of Australia.

Most Chartists stayed at home. There were Chartist associations for ten years or so after 1848. The movement was no longer a threat to the government; there were a few active Chartists, centred round Ernest Jones, who (as another Chartist was later to write) 'kept the old flag flying till he was almost starved into surrender. The pinched face and the thread-bare garments told of trial and suffering. A shabby coat buttoned close up round the throat seemed to conceal the poverty to which the too faithful *adherence* to a lost cause had reduced him.' The last Chartist Convention was in 1858. The name itself was scarcely used after 1860. Some Chartists joined new political organisations that helped to get the vote for working men in 1867 and 1884. Some were alive to join the Independent Labour Party in the 1890s. One old Chartist, W. H. Chadwick, campaigned in the general election of 1906.

But most of the many thousands of Chartists active in the 'hungry forties' took no further part in politics after 1848. The failures of that year disillusioned them. Moreover, their lives were never as bad again. They were still very poor by our standards, but wages were higher and there were more jobs. Many Leicester handloom weavers found jobs in the boot and

A Leicester street, 1861. This is the earliest known photograph of a Leicester street. It had changed little since the end of the Chartist movement a few years before. Notice the costumes, the policeman and the shop

shoe factories that grew in the town in the 1850s. No longer starving, they and others like them in other towns were content to try to improve their lives slowly through trade unions. In the spring of 1849 a Leicester Chartist called George Wray wrote in the 'Northern Star' that there had been hundreds of Chartists in the town, 'but as soon as they got employment they totally forgot their political duties. It appears to me that if they can get as much by working fourteen or fifteen hours a day as will keep body and soul together they are perfectly satisfied.'

16   Some Other Chartists

1. John Frost

John Frost was born in 1784 at Newport in Monmouthshire. His father, an innkeeper, died when he was a small child and he was brought up by his grandfather, a bootmaker. Like Cooper, Frost became a Radical as a young man largely because of his reading. He had a draper's shop in Newport and from 1821 onwards was writing many political pamphlets. One of his attacks on the Town Clerk of Newport led to his

John Frost

conviction for libel; he had to pay £1,000 damages and spent six months in Cold Bath Fields prison. He worked hard for the 1832 Reform Bill but like other Radicals was soon disappointed in it. He attacked both Whigs and Tories as 'two plundering factions who have robbed the people without mercy', and demanded annual parliaments and manhood suffrage.

The Radicals of Newport elected him to the Board of Guardians in 1834, because he promised to hinder rather than help it. He was elected to Newport Town Council too, was Mayor in 1837 and appointed a Justice of the Peace by the Whig government. He was now a fairly rich and respected citizen. But he was still a Radical, and he became a Chartist. He was thus one of the two delegates to the 1839 Convention who was also a J.P., though in March he lost this position because of his Chartist speeches. He became known as a physical force Chartist, but like O'Connor he did not really intend violence. He was bluffing.

The coalminers and ironworkers of the valleys north of Newport had been quarrelling violently with their employers for years. The miners' wages were cut in 1829 and they were often paid 'in truck'. In 1831 the miners and ironworkers of Merthyr Tydfil wrecked the Court of Requests where the accounts of the debts they owed to their employers' shops were kept; they had to be conquered by soldiers. The employers retaliated by sacking all the men who belonged to a trade union, and the workers countered by forming a secret club called the 'Scotch Cattle' to beat up the managers of truck shops and workers who undercut their wages. They also burnt their enemies' houses. They blackened their faces with boot polish to disguise themselves, and attacked at night. By 1839 the 'Scotch Cattle' were Chartists.

Frost was chairman of the Convention when it dissolved in September after deciding to call off the national strike. When he returned home he found that the local Chartists had decided on action. They thought Wales was a good place for an armed uprising because there were so few soldiers there; they hoped that the English Chartists would rise too when they heard the news from Wales. The leaders of the men who wanted a rising were two innkeepers, Zephaniah Williams and William Jones, and an eccentric surgeon called William Price, who was to take command of the Welsh revolutionary army. (Price is mainly famous because his trial for burning his child's corpse legalised cremation. Another Welsh Chartist summed up the general opinion of him by saying that he was 'a fit subject for a lunatic asylum'. Towards the end of his life he was Archdruid at the Welsh National Eisteddfod.)

Frost did not want a rising, but if he took no part he would have felt a traitor to Chartism. He got the others to agree to an armed demonstration, a kind of threatening procession. He was not happy taking part even in this. When he met Dr Price 'he wept like a child and talked of heaven and hell'.

At about 7 p.m. on Sunday 3 November three bands of Chartists set off from different towns to march south to Newport. It was pouring with rain and soon the men were wet through; the Chartists hardly ever had the weather on their side. One band, led by William Jones, turned back, and the other two, led by Frost and Williams, wasted hours waiting for him at the meeting-place outside Newport. They were not able to carry out their plan to occupy Newport before dawn. The delay gave the Mayor time to collect 500 special constables and rush thirty soldiers to the town. They were placed in the Westgate hotel, guarding some arrested Newport Chartists.

Frost's men entered the town and stopped outside the hotel, watching the special constables gathered outside the door. A Chartist shouted 'Give up the prisoners'. A constable shouted back and a scuffle began in which some Chartists seem to have got inside the hall of the hotel. Somebody fired a gun; nobody

The attack on Newport, 1839

knows if he was a Chartist or a constable. Either the Mayor or the lieutenant commanding the soldiers hiding behind the hotel shutters gave the order to fire. The shutters were thrown open and the soldiers fired three volleys at the crowd outside. Between ten and twenty—nobody is sure—were killed. The Chartists were taken completely by surprise and they dropped their guns and fled to their homes. On the way some of them met William Jones and his men, just arriving at Newport. Jones shouted 'Damn me, then we are done', and fled too.

Dr Price managed to get to Paris but the other three were captured in a few days. They were tried for high treason. The prosecution tried to prove that a rising, not a demonstration, had been planned and that the leaders were part of a wider plot to start a much larger revolution in Britain. With his usual generosity O'Connor collected a large fund for their defence and gave a week's profits from the 'Northern Star' towards it. He hired two famous lawyers who were able to tear holes in the prosecution's case. Chartists in other parts of Britain were planning to rise but there is very little evidence that they knew what the Newport men were doing or that their demonstration was to be the signal for a general rising. But the jury found the men guilty and they were sentenced to death, which was reduced to transportation for life at the request of the Lord Chief Justice himself.

Frost, already fifty-six, spent the next fifteen years as a convict in Tasmania. He was well treated at first, but in a letter to his wife he attacked Lord John Russell; the letter got into the press and Frost served two years' hard labour for it, which meant breaking stones in a gang of men chained together. After this he served in a grocery store, and when he got his *ticket of leave* he became a schoolmaster. Many Chartist leaders were teachers for part of their lives.

In 1854 he was pardoned on condition that he lived outside Britain, and for a year he lived in New York and California. He attacked the British ruling class as the 'curse of the world', and described the horrors of convict life. At the end of the Crimean War he was fully pardoned and allowed to live in Britain. He settled near Bristol and lectured up and down the country on his Chartist adventures and his transportation. He died in 1877, aged ninety-three. He never wrote the autobiography he promised, which is a pity; it would be interesting to have his account of the Newport affair and of what it was really like to be a convict in Australia.

2. *Joseph Rayner Stephens*

Some clergymen were Chartists. They sympathised with the very poor men and women they found in their parishes and believed that the Charter was needed to better their lives. The best-known clergyman Chartist was Joseph Rayner Stephens of Ashton-under-Lyne, Lancashire. His father was a Wesleyan Methodist minister and after his education at Manchester

Joseph Rayner Stephens

Grammar School his son became a Methodist minister too. In 1834 he quarrelled with his church authorities and took most of his congregation with him to a chapel of his own. Stephens was an impressive speaker; tall and dark, with a high forehead and piercing eyes, he could hold his audiences spellbound with his sermons. He soon turned to speaking, inside and outside chapel, about political topics on which his religion and his great sense of right and wrong made him feel deeply.

Many Chartists were also active in the Short-Time movement in the North, to limit the hours worked in the cotton and woollen mills by women and children, and men too. Stephens was making violent speeches against 'factory slavery' and the New Poor Law from 1836 onwards, and afterwards he became a Chartist. In a typical speech he said:

'There is not one mill in England that has not been built with gold coined out of the blood and bones of the operatives. Before children of eight years old should be allowed to go into the factory for the purpose of unnatural and killing labour, before they should cross the threshold to be murdered, the door-posts should come down.'

And about the cotton manufacturers:

'We shall destroy their abodes of guilt, which they have reared to violate all law and God's Book. We shall wrap in one awful sheet of devouring flame, which no army can resist, the factories of the cotton tyrants.'

On New Year's Day 1838 he made his most famous speech against the 'vile, fiendish and abominable New Poor Law':

'Sooner than wife and husband, father and son should be sundered and dungeoned, and fed on "skillee", sooner than wife and husband should wear prison dress, Newcastle ought to be and should be one blaze of fire, with only one way to put it out, and that with the blood of all who supported this terrible law.' When all legal means had failed, 'it would be law for every man to have his firelock, pistols, cutlass, sword or pike, and for every woman to have her pair of scissors, and for every child to have its paper of pins and box of needles, and let every man, with a torch in one hand and a dagger in the other, put to death any and all who tried to separate man and wife'.

He was elected delegate to the 1839 Convention and was the first Chartist leader to be arrested for *sedition*. From August 1839 he served eighteen months' imprisonment in Chester Castle. On his release he had to promise to behave well for five years and he left the Chartist movement. But a stronger reason for his doing this was his disappointment with Chartist leaders like O'Connor who did not share his religious approach to politics. It was important to him that men should feel that fighting evil was working for God.

He did continue to attack the New Poor Law and factory conditions, sometimes in newspapers he published himself, 'Stephen's Monthly Magazine', the 'Ashton Chronicle', and the 'Champion'. During the American Civil War he helped the workers made unemployed by the 'cotton famine'. (The blockade of the Confederacy by the Northern States cut off the supply of cotton to Lancashire.) In 1863 he was chaplain to the Miners' Conference in Leeds which founded the miners' trade union, the National Miners' Association, and four years later he helped to begin the trade union campaign in Lancashire for an eight-hour day in factories. He died in 1879.

3. William Lovett

We have already met William Lovett as one of the founders of the first Chartist body, the London Working Men's Association, in 1836, the man who wrote the People's Charter, and the secretary of the first Chartist Convention in 1839.

William Lovett

He was born in 1800 near Penzance in Cornwall. His father, a sea captain, was drowned before he was born and he was brought up by his mother, a strict Methodist. He was apprenticed to his uncle, a rope-maker, but later found that he could not earn a living at that trade because ropes were being replaced by iron cables. We know of this kind of redundancy today but it was common then too. Lovett tried fishing, but was seasick. Fortunately, he was a good carpenter, and earned enough making tea-caddies to get him to London. There he became a cabinetmaker, and, as a result of his reading, became a Radical. Like many other Radicals, he joined the co-operative movement that Robert Owen led, and was a member of the first London Co-operative Trading Association in 1829, the ancestor of the co-operative shops of today.

In the struggle for the Reform Bill he and his friends did not think the Whig bill went far enough and called for manhood suffrage. They used to meet in the Rotunda in Blackfriars Road and were called 'Rotundaists'. They worked hard for the Grand National Consolidated Trades' Union—Robert Owen's attempt to form a vast national union for all workers. Employers dismissed its members; the union hit back by striking but did not have enough money to pay the strikers. The Whig government feared it.

Trade unions were quite legal but six farm labourers of Tolpuddle in Dorset were arrested for making new members of their union branch swear secret oaths of loyalty. Such oaths were illegal under an old disregarded law. The prosecution of the 'Tolpuddle Martyrs' under this law was trickery—as though a modern government were to prosecute people for travelling on a Sunday, which strictly speaking is still illegal. The Tolpuddle Martyrs were transported to Australia for seven years. Lovett was the secretary of the committee that worked hard for their release. The refusal of the Whig government to do so until 1839 helps to explain why the Whigs were so hated by the Chartists. The Grand National Consolidated Trades' Union soon collapsed and their disappointment led many workers to the more forceful methods of Chartism a few years later.

Lovett was a quiet, gentle man, tall, thin and rather melancholy, a good speaker but quite unable to whip a crowd into frenzy as O'Connor did. He was very different from O'Connor in character, and from Thomas Cooper too, in spite of the interest they shared in books and education. Lovett hated O'Connor—the 'great I AM of politics', he called him—and the violence of his speeches—'his Irish boasting about arming and fighting'. Lovett believed in 'moral force' and many writers since Chartist times have regarded this as better, morally, than the threats of violence that O'Connor used in 1839. But in fact O'Connor's policy in 1839 was more sensible. His bluff might have worked but there was no chance at all that the Whigs and Tories in the 1830s would listen to the peaceful and reasonable arguments of Lovett. Moral force would have taken years, but as O'Connor said, 'starving men cannot wait'.

Lovett was courageous. Angry at the riot provoked in Birmingham in 1839 by the police (see p. 23) he protested in the Convention that 'a wanton, flagrant and unjust outrage has been made upon the people of Birmingham by a bloodthirsty force from London'. As secretary to the Convention he signed a poster repeating these words. When it appeared in the town he was arrested. His conviction for sedition followed and he served twelve months in Warwick gaol. The prison was filthy and he was given no fire, even in winter, and little to eat except 'black-beetle', a 'soup in which there was no other appearance of meat than some slimy, stringy particles'. He soon felt ill, and not having the energy or personality which enabled Cooper to make such a nuisance of himself in Stafford, nearly died.

In prison he did manage to write a book, 'Chartism, a New Organisation of the People', which was published on his release. In it Lovett, disgusted with the physical force Chartists, put forward his plans for a great scheme of self-education by which working people could make themselves fit for the vote; how they were to get it when they were educated was not made clear. All the men who had signed the first petition were to be asked to subscribe a penny a week. This would be enough for the creation each year of eighty District Halls (schools for children and adults) and 710 circulating libraries. O'Connor attacked this scheme: 'I object to knowledge Chartism, because it implicitly acknowledges a standard of some sort of learning or education as necessary before a man can have his political rights'. The next thing, he said, would be 'soap and water Chartism', to clean men's necks to make them fit for the vote. Most Chartists agreed with O'Connor, and only one district hall was established.

Earlier in this book the Corn Laws were mentioned. Most Chartists wanted these repealed because they thought that they raised the price of bread. Most middle-class people in towns disliked the Corn Laws too—shopkeepers, traders, manufacturers. In 1838 some Manchester cotton merchants and manufacturers started the Anti-Corn Law League and soon it had branches in towns all over England. There was a branch in Leicester to which many of the stocking manufacturers belonged. To get what they wanted the leaguers used methods very different from those of the Chartists. The rich members of the league kept it well supplied with money—£100,000 in 1844 as against the £1,000 'National Rent' that the Chartists collected in 1839. The league used the new railways to send paid lecturers to meetings all over the country and the new penny post (which started in 1840) to send a packet of anti-corn-law leaflets to every elector. Anti-corn-law slogans were printed on handkerchiefs, teapots, plates and pincushions. Some of the credit for the repeal of the Corn Laws in 1846 should go to the league.

The leaguers thought that repeal of the Corn Laws would mean that Britain would import more foreign corn and that foreigners would then buy British goods in return. The country would be more prosperous and everybody, workers included, would benefit. Most Chartists were suspicious of the league and attacked it. A Leicester Chartist made a speech against the league at the meeting in 1840 that Cooper attended (see p. 1). This account of the speech is taken from Cooper's autobiography.

'Not that Corn Law repeal is wrong; when we get the Charter we will repeal the Corn Laws and all other bad laws. But if you give up your agitation for the Charter to help the Free Traders, they will not help you to get the Charter. Don't be deceived by the middle classes again. You helped them to get their votes. But where are the fine promises they made you? Gone to the winds! They said that when they had got their votes, they would help you to get yours. But they and the rotten Whigs never remembered you. All the reforms of the Whigs have been for the benefit of the middle classes—not for yours. And now they want to get the Corn Laws repealed—not for your benefit —but for their own. "Cheap bread!" they cry. But they mean "Low wages". Do not listen to their cant and humbug. Stick to your Charter. You are slaves without your votes!'

The Chartists thought that the leaguers wanted repeal so that they could lower wages even more. Cooper helped to break up meetings of the Anti-Corn-Law League in Leicester. So did O'Connor in Manchester. Most leaguers hated the Chartists more than the Corn Law; most Chartists hated the leaguers more than the Corn Laws.

But in 1842 some leaguers thought that they should try to

get Chartist support for their movement; it might help it. They turned to Lovett and his friends, the 'respectable' moral force Chartists. Lovett was eager to co-operate; the support of middle-class men might help him to get the Charter. The result was the Complete Suffrage Union, which held its first meeting in Birmingham in April 1842. The leaguers accepted all six points of the Charter. They would not accept the name 'Charter'; it meant to them violence, physical force and strikes. Lovett and his friends would not give up the name that meant so much to them 'to serve the selfish aims of sugar-weighing, tape-measuring shopocrats'. The C.S.U. collapsed, and Lovett, disappointed, dropped out of politics.

He gave up most of the rest of his life to teaching. In 1857 he lost his only district hall; the publican next door wanted his school for a dance hall and 'gin palace'. He tricked Lovett out of his lease. Lovett was the kind of simple, honest man that scoundrels get the better of. He continued to teach until his death in 1876 and wrote textbooks on astronomy, geology and natural history. He died poor: 'Somehow I was never destined to make money.'

17 A Chartist Hymn

This is one of the sixteen hymns written by William Jones, a glovemaker, for the 'Shakespearean Chartist Hymn Book'. It was sung to the tune 'Calcutta'.

'Sons of poverty assemble,
Ye whose hearts with woe are riven,
Let the guilty tyrants tremble,
Who your hearts such pain have given.
We will never
From the shrine of truth be driven.

Must ye faint—ah! how much longer?
Better by the sword to die
Than to die of want and hunger:
They heed not your feeble cry:
Lift your voices—
Lift your voices to the sky!

Rouse them from their silken slumbers,
Trouble them amidst their pride.
Swell your ranks, augment your numbers
Spread the Charter, far and wide!
Truth is with us:
God himself is on our side.

See the brave, ye spirit broken,
That uphold your righteous cause:
Who against them hath not spoken?
They are, just as Jesus was,
Persecuted
By bad men and wicked laws.

Dire oppression, Heaven decrees it,
From our land shall soon be hurled.
Mark the coming time and seize it—
Every banner be unfurled!
Spread the Charter!
Spread the Charter through the world.'

WHERE THE INFORMATION IN THIS BOOK COMES FROM

1. *Writings by Chartists or people who knew them:*

   The life of Thomas Cooper, written by Himself, 1872.

   The Life and Struggles of William Lovett in his Pursuit of Bread, Knowledge and Freedom, 1876. Lovett's autobiography.

   The Practical Management of Small Farms. Feargus O'Connor, 1846.

   The Labourer. A magazine published by O'Connor and Ernest Jones, in 1847 and 1848, about the land plan.

   The Warp of Life: or Social and Moral Threads, DANIEL MERRICK, 1876.

   Leaflets from My Life, MARY KIRBY, 1887.

   Leicester Chronicle. A weekly newspaper.

2. *Books by historians of the present day:*

   The Chartist Challenge, A. R. SCHOYEN, 1958. A biography of Harney and, as well, the best history of Chartism.

   Chartist Portraits, G. D. H. COLE, 1941. Short biographies of leading Chartists.

   Chartist Studies, edited by ASA BRIGGS. Chapters by various writers on Chartism in different areas and towns of Britain, including Leicester. It also has a chapter on the land plan.

   Ernest Jones: Chartist, JOHN SAVILLE, 1952.

   Feargus O'Connor: Irishman and Chartist, DONALD READ and ERIC GLASGOW, 1961.

   Radical Leicester, 1780–1850, A. T. PATTERSON, 1954.

   British Working Class Movements: Selected Documents 1789–1875, edited by G. D. H. COLE and A. W. FILSON, 1951.

THINGS TO DO

1. Can you think of any people in Britain today as unfortunate as the stocking-weavers? If so, write a few paragraphs on what ought to be done for them.
2. Imagine yourself to be a stocking-weaver or one of his children. Write a few pages in your diary.
3. Visit a Chartist land colony, using a large-scale map: the six inches to the mile Ordnance Survey map is the best. Make a book on the colony containing sketches or photographs of the cottages, and a map of the plots and how they are used today.
4. Have you ever met people like Feargus O'Connor or Thomas Cooper in real life? If so, describe them.
5. Imagine that you are delegates to the 1839 Chartist Convention. Hold a class discussion on what ought to be done to make the Charter law.
6. Visit your reference library and find out if it has any copies of local newspapers from August 1842. Read accounts of Chartist meetings and write about them.
7. Make a book with accounts and pictures of things in the 1840s (clothes, social conditions, houses) on one side and accounts and pictures of corresponding things today opposite. Vol. 3 of *Everyday Things in England*, by C. H. B. and M. QUENNELL, will help you with the 1840s.
8. Write the diary of a magistrate or policeman for the third week in August, 1842.
9. Make a model of a weaver's cottage or a Chartist bungalow.
10. Find music to fit the songs and hymns in this book. Sing them.
11. Imagine that you are Cooper or Lovett and write your diary for your life in prison.
12. Make a list of the prices given on p. vi and find out the prices of the same things today. Imagine that you are a stocking-weaver trying to keep a family on 5s 6d a week: draw up a budget for how you would spend the money.
13. Write and act one of these scenes:
    (a) A meal in a workhouse. Charles Dickens's novel, *Oliver Twist*, will help you with this.
    (b) Settlers arriving at a land colony.
    (c) A Chartist dinner in honour of Feargus O'Connor.
14. Write an account of the events of April 1848 in London, trying to be fair to both sides.
15. Find a picture of a street in your town in the 1840s and describe how it has changed today.
16. Imagine that you are Feargus O'Connor and write your diary

for the Kennington Common meeting.

17. Write a Chartist song, to any tune you know, in praise of Cooper in Leicester.

18. In this book you will find mentioned: the Bastille (p. 44), Wat Tyler (p. 69), Garibaldi (p. 75) and Abraham Lincoln (p. 75). Find out why these were famous and think out why they should come into this book.

19. Hold a mock trial, with your class, of two Chartists charged with rioting and burning down a police station.

20. For the whole class: imagine that you are a Select Committee of the House of Commons and enquire into either the lives of stocking-weavers or conditions in a workhouse.

21. Look at the picture of the heading of the 'Midland Counties' Illuminator' on p. 28. Write a few sentences on why you think the newspaper was given this name.

22. Compare the picture of the House of Commons in 1842 on p. 37 with a picture of it today. Make lists of the things that are (a) different and (b) the same, in the two pictures.

23. Look at the slogans being carried by the procession in the picture on the cover and on p. 36. Write a few more slogans that you think the Chartists might have used in a procession.

Note: If you can get hold of a magnifying glass, it will help you to read the small print in the picture on page 28 and the slogans on the cover picture.

GLOSSARY

adherence, loyalty

bastille, originally a prison in Paris. A Chartist word for a workhouse

civil servants, workers in government offices

climbing boys, cleaned the soot out of chimneys by climbing them

commissioners, men sent to find out about a problem and to advise the government on what to do to solve it.

constituency, see *electoral districts*

Corn Laws, Laws limiting the import of foreign corn to try to keep up the price of British corn

cutlers, makers or sellers of knives

cut-up, kind of stocking

delegates, men chosen by their friends to represent them at a meeting

to demoralise, to confuse somebody, or to make him lose confidence

dragoons, kind of heavy cavalry

dulcimer, a harp shaped like a flat box

East India Company, large British company that traded with India

electoral districts, areas into which the country is divided for the election of M.P.s—one (or sometimes two in the 1840s) from each area

fictitious, false

gait, way of walking

grenade, small bomb, usually thrown by hand

gudgeons, small fish, easily caught

guerdon, reward

guerrilla, means 'little war' in Spanish: ambushes, fighting in small groups

hands, workers

hosiers, men who sell stockings

hussars, kind of cavalry

hustings, platform on which people voted before it was secret

inflammatory, usually means likely to set something on fire; in this book it means likely to excite people so much that they will be violent

to ingratiate, to try to make yourself liked by someone

insurrection, revolution, rising

lay preacher, ordinary man, not a minister or priest, who preaches part time

leader writer, man who writes the article containing the newspaper's own opinions

lease, contract to hold land on payment of rent

magistrates, judges, usually for less serious crimes

manifesto, published list of things that a group of people mean to do, or want others to do

metropolitan, belonging to London, the metropolis

mortgaged, offered as security for loan. If the loan is not repaid, the property may be taken by the moneylender

oratory, art of making speeches

paupers, very poor people

pike, kind of spear

polling, voting

purgatory, a very uncomfortable place

quill pen, pen made from a feather, usually a goose's

Radicals, people who want complete political reform and who are not satisfied with slight changes

Riot Act, Act of Parliament forbidding riots: read by magistrates to a threatening crowd to warn them that force will be used if they don't go away

secretary, man who organises a club or political party

seditious, likely to arouse people to *sedition*, that is, to riot or start a revolution

Select Committee, small number of M.P.s, who meet to discuss a particular question

Sergeant-at-Arms, kind of policeman in the Houses of Parliament

skilly, thin porridge

slump, time in which workpeople are unemployed

smallholdings, small farms, allotments

special constables, unpaid part-time volunteer policemen

stave, strong stick

suffrage, right to vote

swarthy, dark-skinned

ticket of leave, permission to live outside prison before the period of sentence has finished

toasts, drinking to people's health and happiness at a dinner

Tories, one of the two political parties in Britain over a century ago: often called Conservatives after 1834

Whigs, one of the two political parties in Britain over a century ago

workhouse, building in which paupers lived and did unpleasant work in return for poor relief

wrought-hose, kind of stocking

yarn, spun thread, ready for weaving or knitting

Yeomanry, unpaid part-time cavalry

WORKING MEN'S COLLEGE

LIBRARY